FOREWORD

La Familia Michoacana or as it is also known, *La Familia*, has emerged as one of Mexico's strangest and most grotesque drug cartels. Its leaders — Nazario "El Chayo" Moreno González and José de Jesús "El Chango" Méndez Vargas — insist they are doing the Lord's work when they discipline teenagers for wearing long hair or spraying graffiti on colonial buildings in the Michoacán state capital of Morelia. However, this syndicate is not content with trying to civilize young people. It captures enemies, who may belong to Los Zetas or another competing cartel, and tortures, dismembers, and decapitates them — often leaving heads in public venues as a warning.

Despite their pious opposition to drug consumption by *michoacanos*, "El Chayo" and "El Chango" have amassed a fortune by importing precursor drugs from Asia and Europe through the Michoacán Pacific Coast port of Lázaro Cárdenas. They have constructed scores of sophisticated laboratories to convert these chemicals into methamphetamines for sale in an expanding U.S. market. La Familia also acquires resources by selling protection to merchants, street vendors, loggers, hotel owners, local gangs, and small-scale drug sellers. Rather than speak in terms of extortion, the shadowy organization insists that it "protects" its clients.

La Familia has recruited members from the ranks of the dispossessed. The North American Free Trade Agreement and the 2008-10 economic recession have left thousands of young people, mostly males, wandering the streets of Lázaro Cárdenas, Morelia, and many of the state's other 111 municipalities. Uprooted from their families, unemployed, poorly educated, and homeless, many of these individuals had turned to drugs, alcohol, prostitution, and petty crime to cope with their dreary lives.

Along come La Familia's recruiters with a message of hope. They say, in effect: "Enter a rehabilitation center, clean up your life, and we will provide meaningful opportunities." Only after a person has shed their addiction are they invited to enter a 2-month program based on periods of silence, intensive Bible study, and exposure to Evangelical-style speakers.

If they complete this training—which is unabashed brainwashing—they receive a job, a salary, and integration into a social group. Meanwhile, they contribute to La Familia's ability to move drugs, especially methamphetamines, through Baja California and Sonora onto the streets of the United States.

La Familia's strength has grown because it has aligned with the Gulf and Sinaloa Cartels against Los Zetas in Tamaulipas and other areas south of the border with Texas. If the three groups enjoy success, they will gain access to Nuevo Laredo, which is the largest portal for the bilateral flow of people, money, vehicles, arms, contraband, and drugs.

Dr. George W. Grayson provides an extremely astute analysis of La Familia, emphasizing its origins, evolution, ideology, leaders, and goals.

DOUGLAS C. LOVELACE, JR.
Director
Strategic Studies Institute

ABOUT THE AUTHOR

GEORGE W. GRAYSON, the Class of 1938 Professor of Government at the College of William & Mary, has made more than 200 research trips to Latin America. He is a senior associate at the Center for Strategic and International Studies, an associate scholar at the Foreign Policy Research Institute, and a board member of the Center for Immigration Studies. He served as a Democratic member of the Virginia state legislature for 27 years and belongs to Phi Beta Kappa. Dr. Grayson lectures regularly at the U.S. Department of State, at the National Defense University, and at universities throughout the United States and Mexico. In addition to preparing a dozen books, as well as monographs for the Center for Strategic and International Studies, he has written *Mexico: Narco-Violence and a Failed State?* (Transaction Publishers, 2009), *Mexico's Struggle with Drugs and Thugs* (Foreign Policy Association, 2009), *Mexican Messiah* (Penn State University Press, 2007), *Mesías Mexicano* (Random House-Mondadori, 2006), *Mexico: the Changing of the Guard* (Foreign Policy Association, 2001), *Strange Bedfellows: NATO Marches East* (University Press of America, 1999), and *Mexico: From Corporatism to Pluralism? (Harcourt Brace, 1998).* Dr. Grayson has written articles for the *Commonweal Magazine,* the *Harvard International Review, Foreign-Policy.com, Foreign Policy, Orbis, World Affairs,* the *Baltimore Sun,* the *Christian Science Monitor,* the *Houston Chronicle,* the *Globe and Mail,* the *Los Angeles Times, Newsday, Reforma* (Mexico City), the *San Diego Union-Tribune,* the *Washington Post,* the *Washington Times,* and the *Wall Street Journal.* He wrote a weekly column for *Milenio Semanal* (Mexico City) and is a frequent commentator on CNN and NPR and affiliate stations. Dr. Grayson holds a J.D. from the College of William & Mary and a Ph.D. from the Paul H. Nitze School of Advanced International Studies of the Johns Hopkins University.

SUMMARY

La Familia Michoacana, also known as La Familia, is one of the most bizarre and deadly cartels in the world. Its Bible-pounding leaders recruit young people from rehabilitation centers, insist that they throw off their dependence on alcohol, drugs, and other addictive substances, and, once clean, apply to join their organization. The novitiates must submit themselves to 2 months of brainwashing that includes scripture readings, exposure to motivational speakers, and long periods of silence and meditation. Upon completing their "instruction," they may become couriers, lookouts, or drivers. Those who show an aptitude for violence are taken in groups of 40 to a wilderness area known as the Jesús del Monte. There, they are directed to shoot, butcher, and cook 15 victims to demonstrate that they are neither squeamish about killing innocents nor repulsed by handling bloody body parts.

The leaders of La Familia—known as "El Chango" (José de Jesús Méndez Vargas) and "El Chayo" (Nazario Moreno González) assure those who successfully complete this exercise that they are prepared to do the Lord's work—that is, safeguarding women, combatting competing cartels, and preventing the local sale of drugs.

This syndicate burst onto the national stage on September 6, 2006, when ruffians crashed into the seedy Sol y Sombra nightclub in Uruapan, Michoacán, and fired shots into the air. They screamed at the revelers to lie down, ripped open a plastic bag, and lobbed five human heads onto the beer-stained black and white dance floor. The day before these macabre pyrotechnics, the killers seized their prey from a mechanic's shop and hacked off their heads with bowie knives while the men writhed in pain. "You don't do something like that unless you want to send a big message," said a U.S. law enforcement official, speaking on condition of anonymity about an act of human depravity that would "cast a pall over the darkest nooks of hell."[1]

This action, the first time that severed heads had been used for completely propagandistic purposes, was designed to strike fear into the hearts of the community. Local lore has it that the five decapitated men were involved in the murder of a waitress/prostitute who worked in the bar and had been impregnated by a member of La Familia. A few days before the ghastly incident, she allegedly refused to have sex with these men, who raped and killed her. La Familia began its own investigation and found these individuals guilty.

The desperados left behind a note hailing their act as "divine justice," adding that: "The Family doesn't kill for money; it doesn't kill women; it doesn't kill innocent people; only those who deserve to die, die. Everyone should know . . . this is divine justice."[2]

Such acts of savagery, combined with the wealth accumulated from exporting methamphetamines (meth) and other narcotics to America, have enabled La Familia to form cells in the major municipalities of Michoacán and in neighboring states. Their strength has fostered what the late historian Crane Brinton referred to as "dual sovereignty" in his classic study, *The Anatomy of Revolution.*[3]

This means that parallel to the elected government stands a narco-administration that generates employment (in growing and processing drugs), keeps order (repressing rival cartels), performs civic functions (repairing churches), collects taxes (extorting businessmen), and screens newcomers to the municipality (employing lookouts). Moreover, while the Mexican Constitution prevents mayors, state legislators, governors, and other officials from seeking reelection, no such provision applies to underground leaders, although bullets from opponents rather than ballots may abbreviate their terms.

La Familia has taken advantage of profound changes that have swept Michoacán, an impoverished state that snuggles against Mexico's Pacific Coast. The North American Free Trade Agreement and recent economic woes have increased the number of unemployed. The U.S. border used to provide a ready escape valve for *michoacanos* attempting to find jobs and send payments back to their home communities, many of which are bereft of males between the ages of 18 and 45. However, the September 11, 2001, terrorist attack; wars in the Middle East; and sky-high joblessness north of the Rio Grande have forced Washington to crack down on illegal crossings at the 2,000-mile-long frontier that separates the United States and Mexico.

Difficulty in earning decent prices for traditional fruit and vegetable crops have led small farmers to turn to growing marijuana, which they sell to the brutal, messianic cartel that may finance the purchase of inputs. Others who faced unemployment work in sophisticated laboratories where the self-righteous syndicate turns imported precursor drugs into meth to sell in the burgeoning American market.

Even though La Familia had surpassed the Colima and Jalisco families in meth sales to the United States, little was known about this shadowy organization whose operatives hid among communities of Michoacanos north of the Rio Grande. In 2007 and 2008, Drug Enforcement Administration (DEA) officials began receiving inquiries from law enforcement agencies on both coasts about "La Familia," a cartel that previously had not come to the attention of most local police departments.

In fact, a multiagency Special Operations Division, comprised of more than 300 agents and analysts from federal, state, and local law enforcement organizations was hard at work on Project Coronado to weaken the Michoacán-based cartel's activities in the United States. Planned for 44 months, the operation culminated on October 22, 2009, and constituted the mightiest blow against a Mexican criminal organization. Coronado involved the arrest of 303 individuals linked to La Familia in the United States, as well as the seizure of 500 kilograms of marijuana, 350 kilograms of meth, 62 kilograms of cocaine, 144 weapons, 109 automobiles, and $3.4 million in cash. According to the U.S. Justice Department, the investigation was spearheaded by an alphabet soup of agencies—the DEA; the Federal Bureau of Investigation (FBI); Immigration and Customs Enforcement (ICE); the Internal Revenue Service (IRS); U.S. Customs and Border Protection; the U.S. Marshals Service; and the Bureau of Alcohol, Tobacco, and Firearms (ATF); as well as attorneys from the Criminal Division's Narcotic and Dangerous Drug Section. In November 2010, during Operation CHOKE HOLD, the DEA and other agencies targeted La Familia's formidable Atlanta-area operations. They arrested 45 people and seized cash, guns, and more than two tons of drugs.

Once a "Lone Ranger" in the drug trade, La Familia has cast its lot with the infamous and powerful Sinaloa and Gulf Cartels in their battle against Los Zetas, founded by ex-Special Forces members who formed the Gulf Cartel's Praetorian Guard before striking out on their own. If La Familia and the Sinaloa Cartels displace the paramilitaries, they will have access to Nuevo Laredo, the major portal for the binational flow of narcotics, money, and weapons.

This monograph examines the profound changes sweeping Michoacán in recent years that have facilitated the rise and power of drug traffickers; the origins and evolution of La Familia, its leadership and organization, its ideology and recruitment practices, its impressive resources, its brutal conflict with Los Zetas, its skill in establishing dual sovereignty in various municipalities, if not the entire state; and its long-term goals and their significance for the United States. The conclusion addresses steps that could be taken to curb this extraordinarily wealthy and dangerous criminal organization.

ENDNOTES - SUMMARY

1. James C. McKinley, Jr., "Mexican Drug War Turns Barbaric, Grisly," *New York Times,* October 26, 2006.

2. This may explain why the death note indicated that they "do not kill women."

3. Crane Brinton, *The Anatomy of Revolution,* New York: Random House, 1938.

LA FAMILIA DRUG CARTEL: IMPLICATIONS FOR U.S-MEXICAN SECURITY

INTRODUCTION

Although spawned several years earlier, *La Familia Michoacana*, or *La Familia*, burst into the limelight on September 6, 2006, when ruffians crashed into the seedy Sol y Sombra nightclub in Uruapan, Michoacán and fired shots into the air. They screamed at the revelers to lie down, ripped open a plastic bag, and lobbed five human heads onto the beer-stained black and white dance floor. The desperados left behind a note hailing their act as "divine justice," adding that: "The Family doesn't kill for money; it doesn't kill women; it doesn't kill innocent people; only those who deserve to die, die. Everyone should know . . . this is divine justice."[1]

The day before these macabre pyrotechnics, the killers seized their victims from a mechanic's shop and hacked off their heads with bowie knives, while the men writhed in pain. "You don't do something like that unless you want to send a big message," said a U.S. law enforcement official, speaking on condition of anonymity about an act of human depravity that would "cast a pall over the darkest nooks of hell."[2]

Until the mid-1980s, before their arrests or executions, major drug lords grew marijuana and poppy plants in Aquila, a municipality with a warm, humid climate a few miles from Michoacán's border with Colima. Proximity to the Pacific Ocean and attractive beaches spurred construction of exclusive clubs like La Privada, where kingpins and their families frolicked in the sand and surf. Observers began referring to Aquila as "the small North" (*"el norte chiquito"*) be-

1

cause local residents earned as much money as their family members working in the United States.[3]

While holding sway in Aquila, La Familia concentrates on the Tierra Caliente, the southern half of the state, which is contiguous to Colima, Jalisco, Guerrero, and Mexico State. Although the Sierra Madre del Sur Mountains pierce this tropical and semitropical lowland before it caresses the coast, the Tierra Caliente is known for producing sorghum, melons, mangos, sugarcane, lemons, and marijuana.[4] La Familia engages in bloody warfare for the control of imports, growing areas, processing plants for synthetic drugs, and transit routes to the United States.[5] The messianic syndicate has also branched out into extortion, kidnapping, human smuggling, contraband, loan sharking, and small-scale sales of marijuana and cocaine.

La Familia's traditional competitors in Michoacán and elsewhere include: (1) Los Zetas, founded by deserters from the Army's Special Airborne Forces Group (GAFEs) and once the Gulf Cartel's Praetorian Guard; (2) the Beltrán Leyva organization, or the Pacific Cartel of the South (CPS),[6] former comrades of the Sinaloa Cartel who have forged situational alliances with Los Zetas; (3) the debilitated Milenio Cartel, or Los Valencias, which is in league with the Sinaloa Cartel headed by the infamous Joaquín "El Chapo" Guzmán Loera and Mayel "El Mayo" Zambada García; (4) the Guadalajara Cartel, led by Ignacio "Nacho" Cornejo Villarreal, a close ally of "El Chapo" and "El Mayo," before the Army killed "El Nacho" on July 29, 2010; and (5) the nearly extinct Colima Cartel, once run by the Amezcua Contreras brothers, who pioneered the production of methamphetamines.

In the past year, Los Zetas' expansion and growing clout has come back to haunt them; the Gulf Cartel has turned on its former paramilitary squad-cum-cartel, and vowed to destroy them. In late 2009, La Familia joined the Sinaloa and Gulf Cartels in a move to liquidate Los Zetas, thus reconfiguring pacts in the north of the country.[7] This loose accord, the so-called "Fusion of Anti-Zeta Cartels" (*Fusión de Cárteles Antizetas*) strives to eradicate Los Zetas, who have links to the weakened Beltrán Leyvas, the badly crippled Juárez Cartel, and remnants of the Arellano Félix Organization (AFO) based in Tijuana. Arrests, killings, and betrayals give rise to kaleidoscopic changes in alliances.

El Chapo Guzmán and Jorge Eduardo "El Coss" Costilla Sánchez, overlords of the Sinaloa and Gulf Syndicates, respectively, sought unfettered control of Nuevo Laredo, Tamaulipas, which reaches to Laredo, Texas, via three international bridges and a rail connection. This corridor is the busiest crossing point for goods, arms, and money leaving Mexico bound for the United States and Canada, and vice versa.

Frequent clashes have pitted the cartels against each other. At the same time, the Mexican Army, Navy, and Federal Police have battled these underworld organizations. As a result, areas of the sun-baked Tierra Caliente and neighboring states have become a no-man's land, where 366 drug-related fatalities occurred in Michoacán alone during 2009 and another 231 deaths took place during the first 10 1/2 months of 2010.

No wonder that at a May 30, 2009, news conference, then-Attorney General Eduardo Mora Medina labeled La Familia as Mexico's "most dangerous" cartel — a designation that could be applied equally to Los Zetas. He based this assessment on the blood-curdling cruelty perpetrated by the shadowy, pious organization; its ability to suborn and terrorize politicians; its

3

spectacular surge in constructing sophisticated laboratories to produce methamphetamines; and its access to high-powered weapons in a state where 10,311 arms were confiscated in 2008—tops in the nation. A "psychosis" of fear has invaded municipalities in this region, including Petatlán, Guerrero, known for its "miraculous saint" Jesús de Petatlán. The pervasiveness of violence and bloodshed in this small town prompted a former mayor to say "this municipality has been Colombianized."[8] In 2009, authorities killed or captured 174 members of the cartel. Meanwhile, various law enforcement agencies and the Army suffered 19 deaths, the most in one day at the hands of any criminal organization since Felipe Calderón Hinojosa launched Mexico's version of the "war on drugs" after swearing the presidential oath on December 1, 2006.[9]

This monograph examines: (1) the profound changes sweeping Michoacán in recent years that have facilitated the rise and power of drug traffickers; (2) the origins and evolution of La Familia; (3) its leadership and organization; (4) its ideology and recruitment practices; (5) its impressive resources; (6) its brutal conflict with Los Zetas; (7) its skill in establishing "dual sovereignty" in various municipalities, if not the entire state; and (8) its long-term goals and their significance for the United States. The conclusion will address steps that could be taken to curb this extraordinary criminal organization.

MICHOACÁN'S CHANGING LANDSCAPE

Figure 1 encapsulates the changes that have affected Michoacán in the last few decades. For the sake of brevity, I will expand only on the political, economic, and social aspects of this transition.

4

Political	International/Economic	Social Welfare	Cultural	Religious
Weakening of the once-dominant Institutional Revolutionary Party (PRI), which controled the governorship from 1929-2002; PRI politicians emphasized informality and the lack of respect for the law; these state executives, like their Democratic Revolutionary Party (PRD) successors, obviously had knowledge of--if not ties to--drug syndicates; yet, PRI governors had the means to control illicit activities that got out of hand by deploying--with the backing of the president and other Mexico City officials--the Federal Security Directorate (DFS), the Federal Judicial Police (PJF) and the Army; with all of its warts and blemishes, the PRI governed more effectively--in terms of providing social services, distributing subsidies, meeting public payrolls, and suppressing violence.	The North American Free Trade Agreement (NAFTA); with the phasing out of subsidies and other protective measures, and imports from the U.S. and Canada dealt a blow to farmers living on communal farms (*ejidos*) and small-scale independent producers who provided food to the domestic market.	Breakdown of the PRI's corporatist system, which--though corrupt and inefficient--provided a social safety net. As mentioned under "Religious," the Roman Catholic Church no longer has sufficient social welfare programs to meet the people's needs.	Many towns in the state have few men between the ages of 18 and 50.	Evangelicals, Pentecostals, and Mormons arrived at a time that the Roman Catholic Church did not have the resources to provide the social support mechanisms that flourished in the past. As Professor James H. McDonald has noted: ". . . the two main institutions that provided a safety net are heavily compromised in their ability to do so now."* La Familia and other cartels moved into this social vacuum, creating jobs in the drug industry, as well as in spin-off businesses, construction, the service sector, security, and transportation.
Increased impunity and mounting instability have sparked conflict between and among cartels; this situation has prompted President Felipe Calderón to dispatch tens of thousands of Federal Police and armed forces to the state, which--in turn--has multiplied accusations of human-rights abuses.	Faced with economic stagnation and unemployment, small farmers migrated to other cities (Guadalajara's *maquiladora* sector) or to the U.S. to seek work; they also created a "reserve labor pool" that could be manipulated by the cartels; meanwhile, there was the emergence of what James H. McDonald calls *techno-caciques*, "well-educated political and economic entrepreneurs with nonlocal connections and aspirations."	Significant contraction in remittances from the state's expatriates due to the "Great Recession" in the U.S.; meanwhile, approximately 30% of the 41,000 michoacanos who returned to their home state for the 2009-10 Christmas holiday indicated they might not return to the U.S.; in 2009, Michoacán received 50 million pesos (approximately $5 million) from the Migrants Support Fund to help returning citizens readjust to their native state.	Influx of goods and services from Mexico's modern sector (and from abroad), including electronic items, Internet cafes, spas, and hotels and restaurants that belong to national or international chains; also new foods have appeared in fast-food establishments and convenience stores.	In addition, La Familia, which emphasizes its *michoacana* roots, has sought to provide not only material benefits, but a sense of community for marginalized young people who may be addicted to drugs or alcohol.
Emergence of the National Democratic Front (FDN), which backed Cuauhtémoc Cárdenas in the acutely controversial 1988 presidential contest. Michoacán now has three active parties: the PRD, an off-shoot of the FDN, the PRI, and the National Action Party (PAN).	A cascade of cocaine via the ports of Lázaro Cárdenas and Manzanillo from Andean nations began in the late 1980s and early 1990s as a result of U.S. interdiction of drug flows into Florida and other Atlantic coast states.	Although traditionally high in Michoacán the use of drugs and alcohol has grown in a state where a methamphetamine pill cost 20 pesos ($1.50) apiece.	The influx of "narco dollars" has greatly inflated land prices, placing the purchase of farms--an important social symbol--out of reach of average citizens. Men who have returned from working in the drug trade in the U.S. are prone to adopt other status symbols such as large homes, new cars, and expensive clothing--well beyond the means of even middle-class *michoacanos*; veteran narcos exercise much more discretion.	The subjection of priests to death threats from cartels reflects the diminished influence of the Roman Catholic Church.

Figure 1. Michoacán's Evolving Social Fabric.

The 1989 creation of the PRD, which captured the Governorship in 2002 (Lázaro Cárdenas Batel) and 2008 (Leonel Godoy Rangel); the latter, whose half-brother is close to La Familia, appears to be linked to narco-trafficking. Godoy's reputation is so bad that his endorsement of a gubernatorial candidate in 2011 would be the kiss of death.	Introduction from Europe and Asia of "precursor" drugs in the late 1990s, which gave rise to the construction of laboratories to process these chemicals into methamphetamines--with the relatively isolated municipality of Apatingán serving as a mecca for these labs.	Increased impunity because of mounting corruption by politicians and their criminal allies, who are no longer constrained by "rules of the game" enforced by the top-down PRI/government hierarchy. The inability and/or unwillingness of the PRD and PAN to punish wrongdoers in their bailiwicks.	The relatively small number of lower- and even middle-class *aficionados* cannot engage in traditional sports like cockfighting because of ever-higher wagers--sometimes thousands of dollars on a single match--by narcos and other nouveau riche.	
Intimidation and/or corruption of mayors and other public figures by La Familia and other cartels.	Sharp growth in commerce through Lázaro Cárdenas, which abounds in single, jobless, poorly housed young men, who are vulnerable to drugs, alcohol, and cartel recruitment. In contrast, the state capital of Morelia and Manzanillo, the port city of Colima, boast thick social networks.	Unprecedented violence arising from competition among cartels for *plazas* in Michoacán, including the creation of deadly arsenals of high-powered weapons.		

*McDonald, Electronic mail to author, January 24, 2010.

Sources: Jerjes Aguirre Ochoa, Professor, Universidad Michoacana de San Nicolás de Hidalgo, interview by author, January 10, 2010, Morelia, Michoacán, and Electronic mail, February 10, 2010; James H. McDonald, "A Fading Aztec Sun: The Mexican Opposition and the Politics of Everyday Fear in 1994," *Critique of Anthropology*, Vol. 17, No. 3, September 1997, pp. 263-292; James H. McDonald, "Reconfiguring the Countryside: Power, Control and the (Re)Organization of Farmers in West Mexico," *Human Organization*, Vol. 60, No. 3, 2001; J. H. McDonald, "The Narcoeconomy and Small-town Rural Mexico," *Human Organization*,Vol. 64, No. 2 (summer 2005, pp. 115-124; J. H. McDonald, "The Cultural Effects of the Narcoeconomy in Rural Mexico," *Journal of International and Global Studies,* Vol. 1, No. 1, November 2009, pp. 1-29; Silvia Garduño, "Alerta a Michoacán retorno de paisanos," *Reforma*, January 9, 2010; J. H. McDonald, Electronic mails to author, January 23-24, 2010.

Figure 1. Michoacán's Evolving Social Fabric. (cont.)

Until the 1980s, the Institutional Revolutionary Party (PRI) dominated national and state politics, and the country's chief executive—at times working through governors—could employ cooptation or coercion to achieve his goals. In 1986, a "Democratic Current" (CD) arose within the self-described "revolutionary party." Among its leaders were Cuauhtémoc Cárdenas, a former Michoacán governor and son of the iconic late president, Lázaro Cárdenas del Río (1934-40), former party chief Porfirio Muñoz Ledo, and others who resonated to an authoritarian welfare state. These leaders championed *intra*party "democracy" and decried the use of the *dedazo* — the incumbent chief executive's "big finger" — to anoint the party's nominee in the next presidential contest.

Most CD stalwarts believed in robust state involvement in an economy that owned 1,150 businesses and encompassed hundreds of social programs. They also supported their party's reliance on three components: a "workers" sector that catered to blue-collar union members, most of whom belonged to the Confederation of Mexican Workers; a "peasant" sector composed of small farmers who lived on communal farms known as *ejidos*; and a "popular" sector made up of teachers, bureaucrats, small-businesses owners, professionals, and intellectuals. Although bathed in corruption, inefficiency, and protectionism, this corporatist regime whose rubric was "Revolutionary Nationalism" fostered stability even as it gave rise to PRI electoral victories, jobs for the party faithful, and a safety net for the poor. In addition, membership in a labor campesino, or popular grouping, helped an individual obtain a job for a relative, a driver's license, credit for a modest home, furnishings for that dwelling, and access to a medical facility for himself or a loved one. The CD feared that increased reliance on free markets, as U.S. President Ronald Reagan, U.K. Prime Minister Margaret Thatcher, and Spanish Prime Minister Felipe González advocated, would undermine the PRI's already shaky scaffolding. They regarded as a heretic Carlos Salinas de Gortari, a neoliberal, the leading member of the Mexican Cabinet, and a strong contender for their party's presidential nomination. Following the consecration of Salinas's candidacy, Cárdenas accepted the nomination of the small Authentic Party of the Mexican Revolution, which eventually cast its lot with the CD and a farrago of leftist groups to form the Democratic National Front (FDN). In an extraordinarily controversial outcome, the government proclaimed Salinas the winner. Nevertheless, Cárdenas carried his home state, demonstrating that millions of citizens were tired of the PRI's top-down, venal rule, and welcomed the formation of the leftist-nationalist Democratic Revolutionary Party (PRD), an FDN offspring.

Opposition to the PRI manifested itself in Michoacán's 1992 gubernatorial election. Salinas lofted the star of Eduardo Villaseñor Peña, 46-year-old pork and banking millionaire. The jowly nominee's lack of a university education and his plodding oratory seemed to be drawbacks as he faced an attractive, seasoned PRD opponent. Still, PRI-sponsored polls found that local citizens were fed up with professional politicians and wanted such an "outsider" as their state's next chief executive.

Villaseñor's selection reinforced Salinas's courtship of the business community, as well as his appeals to the National Action Party (PAN), which the candidate's father had helped found and whose support the chief executive needed for his free-trade initiative with Washington and Ottawa. Villaseñor's wealth and access to contributors obviated the need for the PRI to covertly funnel funds into his political accounts, which he promised to make public after the race.

The PRI standard-bearer garnered 53 percent of the ballots cast to bury his PRD antagonist (36 percent) and three also-rans. Even before the results were announced, the PRD began crying foul despite the prediction of every major poll—including those published in the highly respected *El Norte* newspaper and *Este País* magazine—that the PRI would pile up a landslide.

Failing to win on Election Day, the PRD spearheaded marches, demonstrations, and sit-ins in government buildings in Morelia, the state capital. Such antics did not prevent President Salinas's attending Villaseñor's mid-September inauguration in a tightly guarded convention center on the edge of town. Still, tensions rose. At least six PRD activists died under suspicious circumstances, and protesters prevented the entrepreneur-turned-politician from entering his executive office in the magnificent, 16th-century Palacio de Gobierno. Three weeks later, Salinas yanked the rug from under the freshly minted state executive, whom he convinced to request a "leave of absence." This move enabled the president to name a veteran *priísta* and political fixer as interim governor. Salinas clearly sought to avoid the stark choice between political chaos and the use of force in Michoacán, lest he give ammunition to foes of the pending North American Free Trade Agreement (NAFTA).

Challenges to the PRI bore fruit in 2002 when Cárdenas's son Lázaro "Lazarito" Cárdenas Batel won a term as governor on a PRD platform. Six years later, he was succeeded by another *perredista* luminary, Leonel Godoy Rangel. Meanwhile, in 2006, *michoacano* Felipe Calderón, a major figure in the center-right PAN, defeated candidates of the PRI and PRD to win the presidency, and the chief executive's sister,

9

Luisa María Calderón, is maneuvering to run for the Michoacán governorship in the 2011 election. The debilitation of the PRI shattered the networks that, while infused with corruption, enforced "rules of the game" that constrained violence, curbed impunity, provided services to the faithful, and invested the masses with a tenuous link to decisionmakers.

NAFTA linked Mexico to the global economy, greatly expanded the nation's trade with its continental partners, and served as a magnet for foreign investment. The economic debacle that slammed Mexico in December 1994 — the so-called "Christmas Crisis" — prevented then-President Ernesto Zedillo from his promised modernization of Mexican agriculture through regional development ventures that included an efficient extension service, research into new and improved grains, the establishment of small industries in the countryside, targeted subsidies, and farm-to-market roads. As a result, *ejido* dwellers and small independent producers could not compete with agricultural goods produced by vastly more efficient U.S. and Canadian farmers, who enjoyed generous tax benefits and lavish subsidies.

Poor to begin with, Michoacán suffered stagnation and a sharp rise in unemployment at a time when traditional social safety nets administered by the PRI and the Roman Catholic Church were in tatters. A study conducted in 2007 found that 79 percent of the population lived in poverty: the daily income of 56 percent was less than 100 pesos, and 23 percent earned less than 50 pesos. To purchase the *canasta básica* — that is, food and other essential items — 6,500 pesos per month (209 to 233 pesos daily) were required. Of the state's approximately 4 million inhabitants, more than 1,232,000 lacked basic health-care coverage and sought assistance through the state's overburdened health system; only 364,000 *michoacanos* enjoyed medical insurance. [10]

Twenty years of deteriorating conditions accelerated the flow abroad of Michoacán workers, who had been migrating to California for decades. Men, usually alone or with male counterparts, legally and illegally entered the United States to earn money required to support their families. As a result, many Michoacán towns were divested of men between the ages of 18 and 45.

Males who remained in the state often gravitated to the narco economy, which constitutes far more than growing drugs — that is, "it has a huge multiplier effect in the vast array of other jobs it generates both directly (e.g., transportation, security, banking, and communication) and indirectly (e.g., construction, the service sector, and spin-off businesses)." [11] Some of the women left behind attempted to enter the male-controlled agricultural sector, but cultural norms precluded their participating in the lucrative field of drug-trafficking. Thus, the absence of females in the narco-economy of Buenavista — the name used by anthropologist James H. McDonald to characterize a Michoacán town where he conducted extensive research — underscores "an ironic form of inequality in which women are excluded from a potent, albeit illegal, means of financing empowerment." [12] While many men and women who can afford them drive aging, banged-up Ford and Chevrolet trucks, the showrooms of car dealerships feature top-of-the-line sport utility vehicles (SUVs) and luxury pickups with smoked windows that suggest not-so-hidden wealth. [13] According to a recent estimate, 85 percent of legitimate businesses are involved in some manner with La Familia. [14]

So-called "undocumented workers" had to pay human smugglers known as *polleros* upwards of $1,200 to spirit them into a city like Los Angeles. A respected journalist estimated by late 1995 "slightly more Michoacanos harvest[ed] strawberries in California, pick[ed] apples in Oregon, and work[ed] in construction in Illinois — about 2 million — than the 1.9 million adults who still permanently call the state home."[15] Expatriates from Michoacán led the nation in sending remittances back home. In 2008 they returned nearly $2.46 billion, a figure that surpassed Guanajuato ($2.32 billion), Mexico State ($2.1 billion), Jalisco ($1.94 billion), Veracruz ($1.62 billion), and Oaxaca ($1.46 billion). These amounts fell in 2009 because of the "Great Recession" in the United States, giving rise to even more poverty in Michoacán and other states dependent on resources from abroad; in an ironic twist, "some down-and-out Mexican families . . . [began] scraping together what they . . . [could] to support their unemployed loved ones in the United States."[16] Approximately 30 percent of the 41,000 Michoacán residents who returned home for the 2009-2010 Christmas holiday indicated that they might not return to the United States, and remittances to the state plummeted $80 million during the first quarter of 2010. In 2009 the Mexican Congress allotted Michoacán 50 million pesos from the Migrants Support Fund to help returning citizens readjust to their native state. This figure tumbled to 16 million pesos the following year.[17]

At the same time that NAFTA delivered a blow to Michoacán's small farmers, the trilateral accord spurred the growth of cargo at Lázaro Cárdenas. As discussed later, the port became a magnet for single young men looking for work. If unable to land a legitimate job, they — like small farmers — turned to drugs, alcohol, prostitutes, and crime. The mushrooming city became a recruitment center for La Familia and other cartels.

In addition to foodstuffs, machinery, and electronic goods, drugs entered Mexico through Lázaro Cárdenas—especially cocaine from the Andean nations and precursor chemicals from Asia. La Familia and other syndicates built dozens of sophisticated laboratories to convert these chemicals into methamphetamines—chiefly for export to the United States. Local consumption of narcotics grew, and it became possible to purchase a tablet of "meth" for 20 centavos ($1.50). It is ironic that the import, processing, and sale of drugs has done for Michoacán what NAFTA could not, namely, integrate the state into the global economy.

While most are located in Michoacán, ministerial police discovered a methamphetamines lab constructed and operated by La Familia in Colonia Santa Lucía, in southern Puebla.[18]

ORIGINS AND EVOLUTION OF LA FAMILIA MICHOACANA

Carlos "Carlitos"/"El Tísico" Rosales Mendoza helped pave the way for the formation of La Familia. He originally collaborated with Luis Valencia Valencia and Armando "El Maradona" Valencia Cornelio, the cousins who spearheaded the Milenio Cartel. This syndicate sprang to life in 1985 and carried out operations from Michoacán to Nuevo Laredo, Tamaulipas. An ally of the Sinaloa Cartel, it also operated in a dozen states including Jalisco, Colima, and Baja California, and pioneered the importation, processing, and trafficking of synthetic drugs destined for the U.S. market.

A love triangle ended Carlitos's cooperation with Los Valencias. Although married to a beautiful woman, Rosales Mendoza became livid upon finding out that El Maradona had impregnated his former girlfriend, Inés Hernández Oceguera, with whom Carlitos had also had a child.[19]

In light of this presumed perfidy, Rosales Mendoza vowed to drive the Milenio Cartel out of Michoacán. To help accomplish this goal, he called on his ally, Osiel Cárdenas Guillén, chief of the powerful Gulf Cartel, headquartered in Matamoros, Tamaulipas, below Brownsville, Texas. In 2001, Rosales Mendoza requested that Osiel dispatch members of Los Zetas to help him wage war on Los Valencias. Cárdenas Guillén promptly sent two of his deadliest hitmen—Efraín Teodoro "El Efra"/"Zeta 14" Torres and Gustavo "The Erotic One" González Castro—to lead a cadre of gunmen to battle the Milenio Cartel. This additional firepower emboldened Carlitos to order the execution of "anyone with the name Valencia." In an apparent response to this command, hitmen murdered Ernesto Valencia near Aguililla in early December 2006. This murder was just one of a rash of killings during the month. Long before this alleged execution, Uruapan native "El Maradona" changed the name on his voting credential to "José Raúl Morales Santos," and he and family members fled Michoacán.[20] The Army captured him in Tiajomuleo de Zúñiga, Jalisco, on August 15, 2003.

A top lieutenant of Osiel, Rosales Mendoza created "La Empresa." The other founders were Nazario "El Chayo"/"El Más Loco" Moreno González and José de Jesús "El Chango" Méndez Vargas. Both men had joined Carlitos in his vendetta against Los Valencias. Their number-one enforcer was Arnold "La Minsa"

Rueda Medina, who had served a term for selling drugs in the United States in 1999. His ability to identify Valencia organization members for assassination propelled the former car thief's ascent in La Empresa.[21] Enrique Plancarte Solís handled the acquisition and sale of narcotics, and Servando "La Tuta" Gómez Martínez concentrated on drug activities in Arteaga, Michoacán, and the along the coast of Guerrero and Michoacán.

For several years, La Empresa collaborated with Los Zetas. The latter helped Rosales Mendoza stage an escape at the Apatzingán penal facility in early January 2004. Although 19 inmates made it to freedom, the objective was to liberate five killers, kidnappers, and robbers linked to the Gulf Cartel.[22] During the period of Empresa-Zeta cooperation, Rosales Mendoza and 50 Zetas were less successful in August 2004, when they tried in vain to rescue Cárdenas Guillén from the La Palma high-security prison in Mexico State. Two months later (October 24), Army Special Forces arrested El Carlitos in his luxurious residence in the Colonia Lomas de Santa Maria, Morelia. *Reforma* reported that the criminal offered a huge bribe if he were released. He advised his captors that "they did not know with whom they were dealing because he had a ton of money."[23]

With Rosales Mendoza and Cárdenas Guillén behind bars, Los Zetas continued distancing themselves from the Gulf Cartel. As the cutthroat band began operating independently from their original employers, they pursued lucrative *plazas* in Michoacán and Guerrero — with the port of Lázaro Cárdenas constituting their highest priority.

In reaction to Los Zetas incursion, Juan José "The Grandfather" Farías, leader of the local *Guardias Ru-*

rales, or Rural Guards, took the offensive to keep the outsiders from entering Tepalcatepec on Michoacán's perimeter with Jalisco. Members of this unpaid armed and uniformed Mexican Army auxiliary operated in association with the 43rd Military Zone in Apatzingán. An ally of Los Valencias and the Sinaloa Cartel, "The Grandfather" sought to expel the intruders from his region as if he were a daredevil agent of the French Resistance sabotaging the Nazis. Meanwhile, he was suspected of being a major narco-trafficker in his own right. In retaliation for Farías's opposition, Los Zetas decapitated four of his townsmen on August 8, 11, 17, and 21.

On September 4, 2006, they beheaded cheese maker Raúl Farías Alejandres, a relative of The Grandfather, and his brother, Tepalcatepec's mayor-elect Uriel "El Paisa" Farías Álvarez. A note next to the corpse warned: "One by one you go falling. Greetings to 'The Grandfather.' The Family sends you its best. So long, dudes." Additional beheadings followed.[24]

These executions incited a bloody war between Los Zetas and La Empresa. The latter morphed into La Familia in 2006. Rosales Mendoza's arrest thrust leadership into the hands of Nazario "El Chayo" Moreno González, who had lived in Northern California and whom police had arrested in McAllen, Texas, for drug smuggling in 1999, and José de Jesús "El Chango" Méndez Vargas, who had developed a productive relationship with Cárdenas Guillén that proved important later.

The Grandfather, who heads "Los Farías," owns restaurants, hotels, and orchards. He has dropped out of sight in recent years, perhaps because the Attorney General's Office is investigating his possible connections with Zhenli Ye Gon, a trafficking suspect who is mentioned below.

There is a remote chance that another contingent of La Familia has links to the New Jerusalem millenarian movement. The movement took root in the Michoacán municipality of Turicato in 1973 under the tutelage of defrocked Catholic priest Nabor "Papa Nabor" Cárdenas, who died at age 98 in early 2008. Members of the sect endeavor to avoid the fiery apocalypse by obeying their ecclesiastical hierarchy, attending up to four religious services daily, performing a day of communal work each week, spurning drugs and alcohol, and requiring women to wear ankle-length costumes that blend medieval garb with traditional Indian dress.[25]

The August 2003 arrest of "La Maradona" Valencia Cornelio enabled La Familia to surpass the crippled Milenio Cartel with respect to importing precursor chemicals from Germany, India, Thailand, China, Holland, Bulgaria, Pakistan, and other countries through the port of Lázaro Cárdenas on the Michoacán coast.[26] After receipt of the material, they processed it into methamphetamines for sale to American consumers.

Importance of Lázaro Cárdenas.

The importance of Lázaro Cárdenas derives from its strategic location: Half of Mexico's population lives within a 186-mile radius of this coastal city. Bottlenecks at Long Beach and Los Angeles — in addition to relative proximity to Chicago, Houston, and Kansas City — enabled the city to handle 11.5 million tons of cargo in 2009, second only to Manzanillo (18.2 million tons) on the Pacific Coast. Maersk Sealand, Hapag-Lloyd, APL-Meritus, Cosco Lines, Evergreen, CSAV, CCN, and Hamburg Sud number among the major shipping companies that use the facility, through which 17 percent of U.S.-Mexican commerce moved in 2007. In that same year, 774 cargo ships arrived—a figure that rose to 1,046 in 2008. By 2015, the port will handle six-million containers annually.[27] In preparation for this increased capacity, the government and private firms have improved the highways and railways that serve the city and that run north-south through the center of Mexico. The Kansas City Southern de México railroad operates an intermodal corridor between Lázaro Cárdenas and Kansas City. The terminal was inactive for 10 years until Hutchison Port Holdings took over operations in 2003. A rival port operator, Singapore-based PSA International, owns a minority stake in the giant Hong Kong-based consortium.[28]

Dozens of inlets surround the port to which fast launches and semi-submerged vessels ferry illegal items from ships anchored offshore to the mainland, often under the radar of the Mexican Navy and the U.S. Coast Guard.[29]

Drugs also pour through Manzanillo, a large, busy harbor in Colima state northwest of Michoacán where, in July 2007, the Mexican Navy took control of a Hong Kong-flagged vessel that originated in Taiwan. The ship contained 20,000 kilograms of potassium permanganate, a raw material for manufacturing meth-amphetamines, which had remained undetected at its previous stop, Long Beach.

Zhenli Ye Gon was the "legal representative" of Unimed Pharm Chem México, which, between January 2002 and October 2006 accounted for 291 import shipments valued at hundreds of millions of dollars. The goods entered the country through the Mexico City Airport, Nuevo Laredo, Toluca, Veracruz, Lázaro Cárdenas, Manzanillo, and the Pantaco container depot in the Federal District (D.F.).[30]

A search of the Chinese-Mexican multimillionaire's Mexico City mansion turned up $207 million, which constituted two tons of $100 bills. Also discovered were 18 million pesos, 200,000 Euros, 113,000 Hong Kong dollars, Mexican gold coins, and a trove of jewelry.

Alleging that Ye Gon had imported precursor drugs to produce methamphetamines with a street value of $724 million, Drug Enforcement Administration (DEA) agents arrested him in the PJ Rice Bistro in Wheaton, Maryland, on July 23, 2007, before he could tuck into a meal of codfish and baby carrots. The U.S. Justice Department attempted to extradite Ye Gon to Mexico, where he faces up to 73 years in prison. In early 2010, a federal judge blocked this effort, awaiting evidence of "probable cause" for the Shanghai-born suspect's return.[31]

Even with Ye Gon's machinations, Colima is also an open sesame for drugs along with Lázaro Cárdenas. The headquarters of the Mexican Pacific Naval Force is there; it has half the population (137,842) of the Michoacán port (287,254); and it is a much older city with a thick tapestry of social and family ties. Moreover, Manzanillo has a diverse economy that generates a wide array of jobs. The self-proclaimed "Sail Fishing Capital of the World," it has a thriving tuna industry and boasts attractive beaches and well-protected resorts. Las Hadas (the Fairies) was the luxurious venue for filming the 1979 romantic comedy "10," starring Bo Derek and Dudley Moore.

In contrast, Lázaro Cárdenas, previously named Melchor Ocampo del Balsas, only began to grow after the government constructed the Las Truchas Steel Plant (SICARTSA) and Altos Hornos de México (AHMSA) steel mills, which were sold to private investors in 1991. As a result, the Michoacán port brims with people who are poor, unemployed, deracinated, alienated, single or separated from spouses, and vulnerable to enticements from criminal groups.

Still, Colima Governor Mario Anguiano Moreno, who has a closet full of skeletons, complained that a group called Nuevo Milenio is battling La Familia for control of Manzanillo.[32]

Cucaracha Effect.

In what might be called the "cucaracha effect," Mexico City's *Reforma* newspaper reported that in mid-2007 La Familia began to sign up workers to establish a presence in Guanajuato, which is adjacent to Michoacán. Operatives arrived in Salvatierra, Guanajuato, in February 2008. There they met with "The Lawyer," who sought to broker arrangements with municipal authorities in Salvatierra, Coroneo, Moroleón, and Uriangato, as well as with agents from the now-extinct Federal Investigative Agency (AFI)[33] in Uriangato and Salamanca. By offering attractive salaries, The Lawyer recruited local lookouts, known as *"puntas,"* who alert La Familia to military and police movements. In March 2008, Salvatierra's police captured four alleged narco-traffickers, thus thwarting their bid to commence operations in their municipality. Still, their arrest unleashed a wave of executions that totaled 61 in 2008 and 37 during the first 2 months of 2009.[34]

The newspaper *Milenio* cited the appearance of La Familia in other Guanajuato municipalities: León, Irapuato, Salamanca, Guanajuato City, and Celaya as well as the municipalities of Huanimaro, Pénjamo, Acámbaro, Valle de Santiago, and Dolores Hidalgo.[35]

La Familia has even been reported to be in San Miguel de Allende, a picturesque colonial town that the United Nations Educational, Scientific, and Cultural Organization (UNESCO) has designated a World Heritage Site, and it is also a mecca for American and Canadian retirees, artists, and students. Many of these tourists and residents form a pool of illegal drug consumers. In several of these municipalities, La Familia emulates the Italian Mafia by controlling the small outlets that sell cocaine and marijuana to individuals. When a local distributor refused to cooperate, he was killed.

In the past, Juan José "El Azul"/"The Blue" Esparragoza Moreno, an ally of El Chapo Guzmán, controlled Guanajuato. In a negotiation between capos, El Azul relinquished the *plaza* to La Familia, thus avoiding a lethal confrontation. Dominance in Guanajuato fortifies La Familia's ability to impede its rivals' gaining access to Michoacán.[36]

The syndicate has also extended its reach into Mexico State, where it controls — or has conducted operations in — Ecatepec, Valle de Bravo, Chalco, Ixtapaluca, Toluca (the state capital), and other municipalities. In many of these areas, La Familia has corrupted or intimidated law-enforcement personnel. In early November 2008, 100 local police in Chalco, a meandering slum alive with stray dogs just outside Mexico City, demanded the dismissal of their chief whom they accused of having ties with the deadly organization.[37] Mexico State's Attorney General also cited the commander of the state's judicial police as a possible collaborator after he reportedly received 70,000 pesos per month to provide information to La Familia.[38] By mid-November 2008, local law-enforcement agencies had discovered 13 bodies bearing messages from La Familia.

For example, a note that appeared on the cadaver of Braulio Hernández Zuñiga, bodyguard of the operations director of the Toluca Ministerial Police, said: "If you mess with the family, you should prepare the suit in which you are going to die." ["*Con La Familia no se juega, vayan preparando el traje con el que se van a morir.*"][39] Similar warnings appeared next to corpses in Ecatepec, Coacalco, Naucalpan, Tlalnepantla, Toluca, Tultepec, Zumpango, and Nopaltepec.[40]

Complicating the picture in the state of Mexico is the presence of several cartels competing for the Valle de Toluca and the megacities that ring the D.F.: Los Zetas struggle with La Familia over Toluca and Tlalnepantla: the Sinaloa Cartel, aided by killers in "Los Pelones" band, concentrates on Naucalpan, Tecamachalco, and Huixquilucan; and the Beltrán Leyva brothers, with its allies in Colombia's North Valley Cartel, home in on the Valle de Bravo and Ocoyoaca.[41]

The deadliest single episode took place in or near La Marquesa Park, 30 miles outside of Mexico City, on September 13, 2008. The execution-style slaying of 24 bound and gagged men is believed to have arisen out a battle involving the Beltrán Leyvas and La Familia. They were fighting for control of Huixquilucan municipality, strategically located to the West of Mexico City. Raúl "El R" Villa Ortega, who confessed to participating in the bloodbath, worked for Texas-born Édgar "La Barbie" Váldez Villarreal, once the top hit man for the Beltrán Leyvas, the chief of his own band of killers, and a sinister enemy of the *michoacanos* before his August 30, 2010, capture. The Federal Police also arrested three former Huixquilucan security personnel for the atrocity.[42]

In 2008 callers identifying themselves as members of Los Zetas or La Familia led the way in seeking to extort payments from 96 of Mexico State's 125 mayors. These demands, which were made by cell phones registered in Tijuana and Laredo, came from within the confines of Mexico City's Reclusorio Norte Prison. The amount requested varied between $30,000 and $50,000 depending on the municipality and its location. An extortionist who used the name R4 said that, in return for a deposit in a specified bank account, the mayor's family would be left alone. If necessary, the criminal would provide documents indicating the family's daily routine. Rather than fall for the scam, many officials reported the contacts to the Mexico State's Security Agency (ASE).[43]

In addition, the Michoacán-based organization has been active in the Federal District—with the purported goal of giving this city of 8.5 million people a "social cleansing." The criminal syndicate apparently administered the coup de grâce to nine people during a 28-day period. In early April 2009, police found the bodies of two men who had been tortured and executed in the sprawling, impoverished Iztapalapa borough. Next to the victim, a note warned: "Here we don't permit rapists, assailants, [and] car thieves—Sincerely La Familia Michoacana." La Familia killed four more people in Iztapalapa and three in the Tláhuac borough. Words like "for not paying your debt" ("*por no pagar*") or "rat" ("*ratero*") embellished messages on other corpses.[44]

La Familia has also fought the Beltrán Leyvas (ABLs) for turf in Acapulco and in other parts of Guerrero, especially La Tierra Caliente and nearby areas. After the Navy's Marines killed Arturo Beltrán Leyva on December 16, 2009, his cartel seemed enmeshed in a leadership struggle between Arturo's brother, Héctor, and La Barbie, who had served as plaza boss in

23

Acapulco. Meanwhile, La Familia tried to profit from this apparent disarray by seeking unsuccessfully to take over the affluent San Pedro de la Garza García municipality, a Monterrey suburb whose mayor has allied himself with the ABLs. When asked how La Familia was repulsed, Mayor Mauricio Fernández Garza said: "I have a good team of convincers to make clear that these kinds of incursions won't succeed." In addition to the Beltrán Leyvas, the multimillionaire city chief has created a shadowy "group of ruffians" to keep order in his jurisdiction.[45]

This setback notwithstanding, in mid-March 2010, Guerrero became a war zone—with the violence concentrated in Acapulco, Altamirano, Chilpancingo (the state capital), Coyuca, Iguala, and Petaltán. Municipalities targeted for takeover by La Familia included Petatlán, La Unión and Teniente José Azueta—with 43 deaths registered in 2 days.[46] Cuernavaca, too, has suffered a wave of unprecedented violence, beheadings, terror-like threats, etc., which forces many businesses to close early.

LEADERSHIP AND ORGANIZATION

In addition to El Chayo Moreno González and El Chango Méndez Vargas, the founders of the cartel included Enrique "La Chiva" Plancarte Solís and Servando "La Tuta" Gómez Martínez. Rueda Medina served as the right hand of Moreno González.

Little is known about El Chayo, who was born in Apatzingán, Michoacán, on February 28, 1974. As a teenager, he worked in California's Central Valley, and at age 20 spent time in jail in McAllen, Texas, on a minor drug-smuggling charge. One admirer said that he looked like someone who could have ridden with

Zapata.[47] El Chango, who was born in Uruapan, Michoacán, on March 6, 1964, began criminal activities as the right-hand man for a lieutenant of Osiel Cárdenas Guillén, kingpin of the Gulf Cartel. He reveres Cárdenas Guillén, who helped teach him the drug business, as his mentor.

El Chayo and El Chango, considered respectively the "brawn" and the "brains" of the syndicate, each has responsibility for approximately half of Michoacán: Morelia and the eastern portion of the state constitute the domain of Moreno González; and Lázaro Cárdenas and the western region rest in the hands of Méndez Vargas. The two men have a frosty relationship, and El Chango warns his men not to fraternize with subordinates of El Chayo whom they look down upon because, unlike Méndez Vargas, he has limited knowledge of the narcotics business. The message is, more or less, "You can help them change a tire, but don't party with them."

La Familia dominates narcotics sales in the lion's share of Michoacán's 113 municipalities. Lázaro Cárdenas, Arteaga, Apatzingán, Uruapan, Nueva Italia, Morelia, and other important venues have a single plaza boss. Many of the 25 to 50 plaza chiefs have responsibility for half a dozen or so small municipalities. Each plaza leader has an enforcer, who takes care of extortion and other strong-arm activities.

Enrique "Kiki" Plancarte Solís, who reports directly to El Chayo, is an extremely important member of the hierarchy. He has responsibility for coordinating drug sales to the United States.

La Tuta.

Of all the leaders, the most information is available on Gómez Martínez, who maintains a relatively high profile and serves as the syndicate's chief spokesman.[48] Information from both "Carlos," a protected witness, and Luis Felipe "El Güicho" Gómez Martínez, La Tuta's brother, provides a glimpse into the background on one of the five most important figures in La Familia.

A native of Arteaga, in the mid-1980s at age 19, he and his wife moved to Quiroga, near Morelia, where he was an elementary school teacher. When the couple separated, he went to live at "Medina," his father's ranch outside of Arteaga. For 2 years, he cultivated papayas, tomatoes, and corn. He next taught children on several ranches and, in the process, developed ties to narco-traffickers in the area. "I told Servando not to get mixed up in such activities . . . and that's when he told me that he was involved in the drug business," according to his brother, El Güicho.[49] "I must continue in this because I am unable to escape [*salir*]" was the response."[50]

Whether fact or faction, La Tuta reportedly began relying on Juan Víctor "El Brujo"/"The Witch" Fernández Castañeda, his personal "sorcerer," who used tarot cards to advise him on places to hide from the police, the names of traitors to La Familia, and appropriate operations to undertake. In September 2007 or in early 2008, the wizard claimed that an Arteaga upholstery shop employee had squealed on La Tuta to the military. The crime boss dispatched two hitmen — Genaro "El 17"/"El Cholo" Orozco Flores and Jorge "El Rojo" Fuente Maldonado to eliminate the alleged informer who was relaxing in his own home.

In addition, Fernández Castañeda, who joined La Familia in 2007, continually communicated in person or by telephone with La Tuta, acted as a lookout, took part in money laundering, wrote checks on his boss's Bancomer bank account, and even sent gifts to women with whom Martínez Gómez lived. Federal Police arrested "El Brujo" in Arteaga on August 17, 2009, along with La Tuta's mother, María Teresa Martínez Castañeda; his brother, "El Güicho"; and two other accomplices. The Attorney General's Office released Señora Martínez Castañeda for lack of evidence after 2 days; the four men were imprisoned in Matamoros.

On January 28, 2009, Federal agents captured La Tuta's son, Luis Servando Gómez Patiño, at a cockfight in Arteaga. He was charged with participating in organized crime. La Tuta's brother, Flavio Gómez Martínez, a powerful figure in Arteaga and a financial operator, remains at large. [51] The involvement of La Tuta's son and one or more of his brothers indicates the family ties that permeate the syndicate. In late July 2010, Jalisco authorities arrested Valdemar "El Bombón"/"El Once" Hernández Barajas, 20, who lives with the niece of La Tuta, his political mentor. He was accused of killing one and wounding four police officers. His second nickname, which means 11, derived from his membership in a group known as "The 12 Apostles of Señor Nazario Moreno." [52]

According to Mexico's Ministry of Public Safety (SSP), La Tuta had four confidants, two of whom are at large: Julio César Godoy Toscano, Governor Leonel Godoy Rangel's half-brother, a successful PRD congressional candidate in the July 5, 2009, election, who temporarily turned his seat over to an alternate, and a key mover in Lázaro Cárdenas, Arteaga, and Nueva Italia; and Saúl "El Lince" Solís Solís, a PVEM (Green

Party) nominee for Congress from the Apatzingán area, first cousin to organization leader "Kike" Plancarte Solís, an operator in La Huacana region south of Uruapan, where he maintains contacts with business and political leaders. The two under arrest are Enrique Jorge Alberto "El Gordo" López Barrón, and "El 17" Orozco Flores, who is believed to have been the most trusted bodyguard of "La Tuta."[53]

In early 2010, La Tuta was prepared to marry Lourdes Medina Hernández, a 24-year-old beauty from Arteaga whom he had courted for 3 years. The couple had even acquired property in Nueva Italia. The late July 2009 arrest of Medina Hernández chilled these wedding plans.[54]

In mid-July 2009 Gómez Martínez shocked television journalist Marcos Knapp by phoning into his program, *Voz y Solución*. After introducing himself, La Tuta explained that La Familia "admires President Calderón" and "respects the Army and Navy 100%" because they are performing their duties. Their animus was toward Public Security Secretary Genaro García Luna and his "followers" in the Federal Preventive Police and the Specialized Investigation of Organized Crime intelligence agency (SIEDO) "because they are attacking our families" whom we are committed to defending. He claimed that García Luna was protecting Los Zetas and the Beltrán Leyvas. There are "mafias and criminals everywhere," he affirmed, "and if we don't protect our people the best we can, Los Zetas will come in. . . ."[55]

La Tuta claimed that he wanted to return to the life of a simple teacher and that his organization sought to reach "a consensus" . . . "a national pact" with the government. Otherwise, he stated, "this [the violence] will not halt. . . ."[56] What he implied was that if authorities allowed La Familia to operate with impunity, the organization would rid the state of other cartels, dirty policemen, and other unsavory elements. It appeared that he was seeking a return to the "Pax Mafiosa" of the last third of the 20th century when the government and the cartels established rules of the game that could enrich all parties to the accord. He signed off with the ambiguous words: "God bless everybody, and let God give us the opportunity to live just a little longer. That's all. Thank you."[57]

Mexico City rejected his overture. Then-Interior (Gobernación) Secretary Fernando Mont Gómez, averred that the government "combats equally all criminal groups, without distinction, with the conviction that the only option for their members is to obey the law."[58] Several weeks after Los Zetas or other assailants killed and buried 18 Michoacán tourists in Acapulco in October 2010, La Familia pledged to "dissolve itself" if the government eliminated other cartels in the state. Authorities turned down this ploy, which was designed to stress both the organization's concern for the welfare of michoacanos and their presence as the only local force battling the hated Zetas.

When a New York grand jury indicted Gómez Martínez for conspiracy to import and distribute cocaine and methamphetamines, it also charged brutal activists Ignacio Andrade Rentería, commonly called "Los Cenizas"/"The Ashes," because he has burned so many people to a crisp; his brother, Rigoberto Andrade Rentería; and another Family member.[59]

Like los Zetas, the militaristic cartel centered in Tamaulipas, activists in La Familia sometimes wear uniforms, carry arms, and drive vehicles similar to those of the Mexican Federal Police. This allows them greater freedom to move around their areas of interest.[60] Moreover, leaders of the group have become so brazen that they have designed their own outfits to mark their identity and distinguish their members from adversaries. They treat informants with grotesque cruelty. In April 2009, they murdered at least 14 people in Lázaro Cárdenas. Authorities found the bullet-riddled body of a 35-year-old man whose hands had been tied behind his back and a black plastic bag wrapped and taped over his head. A note next to his corpse warned: "This is what happens to informants of the Z [Zetas], sincerely, La Familia."[61]

The journalist Ravelo also reported that the organization has an executive council composed of businessmen and government officials, along with narco-traffickers from regional and municipal cells.[62]

The La Familia factions include:

- "The Historic Ones" ("*Los Históricos*"), who had or have links with Los Zetas;
- "The Extortionists" ("*Los Extorsionistas*"), composed of businessmen and growers who extort money;
- "Debt Collectors" ("*Los Cobradores de Deudas*"), who are allied with the Milenio and Sinaloa Cartels and who traffic in methamphetamines;
- An unnamed group that concentrates on selling pirated films, DVDs, computer software, and video games;[63]
- "The New Administration" ("*La Nueva Administración*"), whose cell members kill for the cartel; and,
- "*Los Yonqueros*," who carry out kidnappings in Mexico State and the D.F.[64]

A gang called "Los Jaguares" has also assisted La Familia with kidnappings in the Michoacán municipalities of Morelia, Maravatío, Ciudad Hidalgo, and in the Mexico State municipalities of El Oro and Jilote-pec.[65]

United Nations' (UN) security adviser, Professor Edgardo Buscaglia, draws the improbable conclusion that these figures represent a virtual Potemkin Cartel; that is, the real power behind La Familia is the economic structure of the region. "We are confronting a group of criminals that hide behind . . . businesses in which famous politicians and politicians whose names regularly appear in magazines," he said without mentioning names. "Thus we cannot be sure that El Nica [Nicario Barrera Medrano/*plaza* boss in Uruapan], El Chayo or El Chango Méndez is the Head Honcho. The visible chiefs are only screens, the true ones [chiefs] are not visible and they, by dispatching orders, are those who configure the strategies of these mafias. Those whom we see are merely operators."[66]

Miguel Gallardo López, president of the Michoacán employers' confederation COPARMEX, which embraces more than 500 enterprises, rejected Buscaglia's thesis. "Today we see that organized crime has infiltrated all structures but I definitely do not believe that it has reached those levels [in the business community]."[67] A journalist described Michoacán as the "central Pacific coastal state [that is] known on the tourist trail for its colonial cities and exuberant indigenous culture that carries the Day of the Dead ceremonies to levels of intensity seen nowhere else in Mexico."[68] On the one hand, La Familia exploits the poverty that suffuses their areas of operations; at the same time, they launder money by interpenetrating businesses as owners or silent partners. Such "dirty" firms have an advantage over their competitors, which incur higher costs as a result of extortion because they face threats to property, kidnappings, and a loss of revenues, par-

31

ticularly from a sharp downturn in tourism. Dirty money also enables cartels to subsidize their firms.

Figure 2 indicates the key members of La Familia. Appendix 2 furnishes a more expansive list of present and former leaders, specialized operators, and notable apparatchiks.

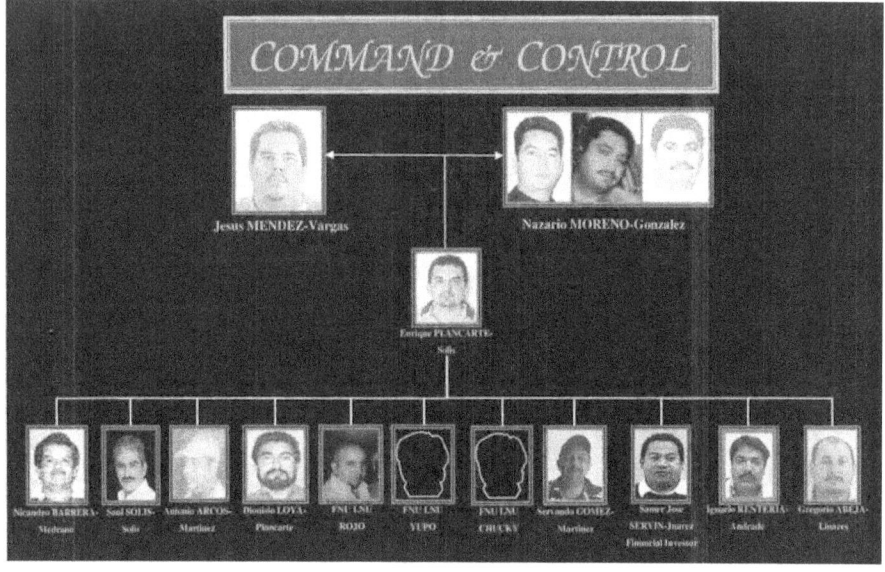

Figure 2. Structure of La Familia Michoacana.

Erroneous reports indicated a possible fragmentation of the cartel when La Familia recruited former members of the armed forces known as "Sierras." A Guatemalan prisoner told SIEDO that the leader was "Sierra One," the second-in-command was "Sierra Two," etc. Other alleged operators carried such fanciful sobriquets such as Sierra Jupiter and Sierra Raven. Each chief supposedly managed a unit of 22 to 30 men, who were responsible for patrolling and monitoring movements in the municipalities under La Familia's domain.

The Sierras got too big for their olive-green pants. Their top leader—Sierra 22—was serving as La Familia's enforcer, under plaza chief Hilario "El Gato" López Morales, in Zitácuaro. The ex-soldier began terrorizing the local population through brutal killings, car thefts, and pressuring a hotel owner to give him the deed to his property. When El Gato found out, he alerted Arnoldo "La Minsa" Rueda Medina, the right-hand man of "El Chayo" Moreno González and "coordinator of coordinators" for La Familia. Rueda Medina convened a meeting of the two top Sierras in Tamaulipas, dressed them down for alienating the local population, and proceeded to have both of them and their comrades killed. He then made certain that stolen automobiles, the hotel deed, and other pilfered items were returned to their rightful owners. Finally, he allowed El Gato to resume control of Zitácuaro and placed Ricardo "El Yankee" Pérez Rivas, a trusted ally, in the plaza's number two position.

La Familia reinforces morale by heaping retribution on authorities who pursue their leaders. The organization swiftly mounted a synchronized counterattack when Federal Police captured Rueda Medina for importing precursor chemicals and dispatching synthetic drugs, cocaine, and marijuana to the United States. He also controlled *plazas* in at least seven states and took the lead in identifying and executing members of Los Zetas and the Beltrán Leyva brothers.[69]

In light of La Minsa's pivotal position and popularity within the rank and file, his comrades struck with a vengeance. They precipitated 4 days of mayhem. On July 11, 2009, La Familia ambushed units of the armed forces and Federal Police in eight cities, beginning with Michoacán's capital, Morelia. On July 12, a major confrontation erupted in Lázaro Cárdenas, but La

Familia also used high-powered rifles and fragmentation grenades against its foes in neighboring Guerrero and Guanatuato states. On July 13, the cartel captured, stripped, bound, and executed a dozen Federal Police, leaving their corpses in a heap alongside the Morelia-Lázaro Cárdenas Highway with a message reading: "Come for another [of our leaders], we are waiting for you." (" *Vengan por otro, los estamos esperando* "). On July 14, La Familia ambushed a tourist bus carrying 30 Federal Police near La Huacana on the same highway. Later that day, it set fire to the Federal Police headquarters in Zitácuaro.

The prolonged battle extinguished the lives of at least 17 Federal Police and two soldiers, a 1-day record under Calderón's 2 1/2-year old administration. Twenty or more civilian and military agents of the federal government suffered wounds. Two members of La Familia perished in what some journalists hyperbolically called Mexico's version of the "Tet Offensive" — an early 1968 communist onslaught that failed militarily, but convinced opinion leaders such as the late television journalist Walter Cronkite that America could not win the Vietnam conflict.

Calderon dispatched 5,500 soldiers, sailors, marines, and police, who erected checkpoints on major arteries and shored up redoubts in La Familia strongholds. Local citizens exhibited a mixed reaction to the influx of men hefting automatic weapons and wearing ski masks. Gerardo Gómez, a Morelia resident, told a *Reuters* reporter: "We've reached a point where the local authorities are tapped out, and so unfortunately it's necessary to call in extra forces to try and restore peace."[70]

Meanwhile, Sonia Sánchez, a lime farmer in the town of Buenavista, told a *Washington Post* correspondent that people were "furious" over the apprehension of their mayor, Osvaldo Esquivel Lucatero, a physician and soccer coach. Citizens protested his incarceration by chaining shut the doors of the municipal building.

IDEOLOGY

In contrast to Los Zetas and other Mexican capos, La Familia's leaders—especially Nazario "El Chayo" Moreno González—assert that it is religiously motivated to a degree that approaches messianic zeal. It claims to administer "divine justice" to rapists, robbers, corrupters of youth, and others whom the syndicate deems undesirable. It has even harshly treated teenagers caught spraying graffiti on colonial buildings in Morelia or youngsters, back from the United States, who wore hairnets and overly large, low-slung pants.[71] Some mothers praise the cartel for disciplining their unruly teenagers—especially the so-called *"Los Ni Nis,"* who neither study nor work. Cartel leaders have pledged to: "Eradicate from the state of Michoacán kidnapping, extortion in person and by telephone, paid assassinations, express kidnapping, tractor-trailer and auto theft, [and] home robberies done by people like those mentioned, who have made the state of Michoacán an unsafe place. Our sole motive is that we love our state and are no longer willing to see our people's dignity trampled on."[72]

The organization displayed a determination to safeguard women in its public debut when it bowled the heads onto the dance floor in Uruapan in September 2006. This action, the first time that severed heads had been used for completely propagandistic purposes, was also designed to strike fear into the hearts of the community. Local lore has it that the five decapitated men were involved in the murder of a waitress/prostitute who worked in the bar and had been impregnated by a member of La Familia. A few days before the ghastly incident, she allegedly refused to have sex with these men, who raped and killed her. La Familia began its own investigation and found these individuals guilty. This may explain why the death note indicated that: "La Familia doesn't kill for money, doesn't kill women, doesn't kill innocent people. It only kills those who deserve to die."[73]

In late January 2010, La Familia whipped with barbed wire and boards six presumed criminals in Zamora, Michoacán. After the sustained torture, it forced the men to walk in silence around a busy traffic circle for more than 30 minutes with signs reading: "Keep an eye out you rats, we are coming for you, sincerely La Familia," "I am a rat and La Familia is punishing me," "This is for all the rats and 'recatos', sincerely La Familia Michoacana," and "This is for all delinquents, La Familia is here citizens, don't judge us, we are cleaning your city." After this episode, the young men avoided talking to police and the media, while refusing medical attention.[74]

One careful observer learned of a similar form of "social messaging" in Zamora, a mid-size municipality in the Northwest area of Michoacán, where "groups of flagellants had appeared . . . men with the shirts pulled up or off and their backs whipped raw. The men chanted and carried placards denouncing themselves as thieves and rapists. Some of the placards were signed 'La Familia'." [75]

Proceso magazine's Richard Ravelo insists that the 4,000 members of La Familia were born and raised in Michoacán, attend church regularly, carry Bibles, and distribute the Good Book in local government offices.[76] It is unclear whether these are King James versions of the Bible or ones that have been embellished by the teaching of La Familia's own leaders. They even justify executions as "orders from the Lord."

Indoctrination.

La Familia stalwarts focus their evangelical appeals on young people who are poor and marginalized. They emphasize rehabilitation, empowerment, and self-renewal for drug addicts, alcoholics, glue-sniffers, juvenile delinquents, and others who feel alone, isolated, and abandoned. In fact, the organization operates a dozen or more rehabilitation centers, which give immediate access to recruits. Of Michoacán's 4.7 million residents, 224,270 young people aged 12 to 25 are addicts, with cocaine being the substance of choice. There are at least 2,100 points of sale for drugs in the state.[77] The syndicate castigates the use of alcohol, tobacco, and drugs even as it preaches family cohesion to raise members' motivation and spirits and respect for women. In addition, the organization has created "Youth: Art and Culture" ("Jóvenes: Arte y Cultura"), a group that attracts teenagers into its ranks in the Tierra Caliente and Guerrero.

To begin with, the recruits must clean up their lives by throwing off any drug or alcohol addiction they may have. Before his April 2009 arrest at a baptism, Rafael "El Cede" Cedeño Hernández, a self-described pastor and an observer on the state's human rights commission, took charge of indoctrination. He designed the

6- to 8-week intensive educational programs, selected the texts and videos used as part of this brainwashing, and required periodic vows of silence by the class members as if they were religious brothers and sisters. Days without talking supposedly enhanced spiritual concentration and facilitated the individuals' sense of solidarity, thankfulness, altruism, and complete loyalty to La Familia's leaders. Caricatures represented the three stages in the neophytes' right of passage. The first portrayed anger and deception ("Así venía"); the second revealed interest [in changing one's life], ("*Me interesé*") and the third depicted total joys ("*Así salí*"). La Familia has sponsored seminars by Carlos Cuauhtémoc Sánchez and inspirational speaker Miguel Ángel Cornejo in Morelia. Events may resemble Oral Roberts-type evangelical services, and El Cede claimed to have brought 9,000 people into the fold.[78] Some converts allegedly indulge in self-ornamentations — namely, wearing a crucifix and a bracelet made from a rosary — to demonstrate their rebirth.[79]

El Milenio newspaper reported that La Familia uses the works of American counselor John Eldredge to instruct and motivate their teetotaler recruits. Unlike La Familia, Eldredge does not espouse violence and "has never had any contact with La Familia or its representatives."[80] Founder of the Ransomed Heart Ministries in Colorado Springs, Colorado, Eldredge has written that: "Every man wants a battle to fight, an adventure to live, and beautiful rescue." The "big message" of his "small ministry" is "to set men and women free to live from the heart as God's intimate allies . . . That's what we are devoted to — seeing men and women come fully alive as the image-bearers of a breathtaking God."[81]

The Christian author preaches a gospel that combines the rugged vigor of Teddy Roosevelt, the élan of Jesus expelling money changers from the Temple of Solomon, and the bravery of Moses leading the Israelites out of bondage. In his book, *Wild at Heart*, which, like many of his writings, has been translated into Spanish, he proclaims that "God created man to take risks."

His treatment of Samson provides insights into his philosophy:

> Remember that wild man Samson? He's got a pretty impressive masculine résumé: he killed a lion with his bare hands, pummeled and stripped 30 Philistines when they used his wife against him, and finally, after they burned her to death, he killed a thousand men with the jawbone of a donkey. Not a guy to mess with. But did you notice? All those events happened when *"the Spirit of the Lord came upon him"* (Judg. 15:14 emphasis added by Eldredge).[82]

Eldredge demonstrates a fascination with white he-men in Hollywood movies. "Beyond being alpha males, there are also hero-saviors."[83] His favorites include *Braveheart, Flying Tigers, The Bridge on the River Kwai, The Magnificent Seven, Shane, High Noon, Saving Private Ryan, Top Gun*, the *Die Hard* films, *Gladiator* — "the movies a man loves reveal what his heart longs for, what is set inside him from the day of his birth. Like it or not, there is something fierce in the heart of every man."[84] No doubt La Familia's evangelists adapt Eldredge's writings to their situation, even as they probably show all or parts of films that he prizes.

Moreno González, the most ostentatiously religious of the leadership, has prepared a catechism that all present and potential cartel members must read.

It is called *"Pensamientos de la Familia"* ("La Familia's Maxims") and is signed by "El Más Loco." These tenets, which have gone through several editions, mirror the "Be-all-you-can-be" teachings of John Eldredge.[85]

A growing evangelical strategy in the United States involves stressing violent sports such as kickboxing, wrestling, and other martial arts to convey the idea that Christ fought for his beliefs and that Christianity has become too feminized. The Xtreme Ministries, a small congregation near Nashville, Tennessee, is one of approximately 700 white evangelical churches that emphasize this muscular approach to promoting Christian values, quoting scripture like "fight the good fight" from Timothy 6:12. "I'm fighting to provide a better quality of life for my family and provide them with things that I didn't have growing up," said Mike Thompson, a 32-year-old former gang member who competes under the nickname "The Fury." "Once I accepted Christ in my life," he added, "I realized that a person can fight for good."[86]

In return for their complete devotion, La Familia pays its lookouts U.S. $190 to $230 per week.[87] These are princely salaries in a state where unemployment is soaring even as tourism nosedived 40 percent in 2009 only to recover slightly in 2010. José Luis Piñeyro, an analyst who is close to the Mexican armed forces, believes that joblessness and poverty are creating "an army in reserve" for the traffickers.[88] Disobeying La Familia's code of conduct yields a beating for the first infraction; a more severe thrashing for the second offense; and execution for the third violation. The syndicate keeps careful records of members' families in order to take reprisals against them if an activist deserts or fails to carry out a mission. The organization's perverted rules also decree that "whoever leaves La

Familia dies." Although the circumstances surrounding his death are not known, Family operative José Luis "El Jaguar" Carranza Galván was found with 18 bullet holes in his body in Ecatepec on November 23, 2008—an apparent victim of his erstwhile comrades in arms.[89]

Meanwhile, La Familia trumpets such social works as rebuilding schools, contributing to churches, and extending credits to farmers and businesses. Like the Mafia, La Familia professes to bolster grassroots support through acts of beneficence. To that end, it avows that it extends credit to farmers and businesses, builds drainage systems, lays out volleyball courts, constructs schools, erects street lights, donates books, prevents the sale of adulterated wine, collects debts owed to local residents, and employs "extremely strong strategies" to bring order to the Tierra Caliente.[90] "If you were sick and had no money, they'd take you to the hospital and pay for medicine. If you couldn't afford tortillas, they'd buy some for you," claimed Veronica Medina, a sympathizer of La Familia who is also known as the "Queen of the South" after the title of a popular Spanish novel about narco-trafficking in Mexico.[91] Thus, La Familia is a contrast to the Milenio Cartel, which has recruited outsiders called "antizetas."[92] The author found few examples of such civic endeavors in Michoacán.

The Reverend Andrés Larios, a young priest who grew up in the Tierra Caliente, has established a youth group, "The Rainbow," to counter La Familia's appeals to those adolescents who seek to become drug dealers. "They say traffickers have the prettiest wives, the best houses in town, and the best cars." Other young people have told Larios that they are enmeshed in organized crime and must continue these activities to supplement their family's income.

Father Andrés attempts to connect with the 100 or so teenagers who have signed up for Catholic extra-curricular education each year. He arranges basketball tournaments, resonates to the same movies and music they prefer, and adorns his office with pictures of him sporting fashionable sunglasses and riding a jet ski, making him "resemble a cool older brother rather than a stereotypical local priest." "We understand each other," he says. "I speak their language." Local narcos have warned him not to talk about the drug trade, and one even told him to conduct mass at his ranch — or else. "Sometimes living here gives us a feeling of impotence," he admits.[93]

Narco-banners.

The syndicate also posts so-called "narco-banners," which blast the presence of other organizations in their state. Newspapers and TV stations invariably run pictures of these signs, which magnify the coverage they receive. Typical of their "Michoacán for the *michoacanos*" is the message:

> PFP [Federal Police]-Zetas get out of Michoacán. Michoacán is for *michoacanos*. Respect them and you will be respected. Don't pay attention to your chiefs and, better still, leave. You are not welcome in Michoacán. Sincerely La Familia Michoacana.[94]

By avoiding the term "cartel," La Familia endeavors to present itself as a community-oriented organization — like the Red Cross, Caritas, or the Salvation Army — that lends a hand to those in need. Cartel big shots stress that all members are *michoacanos*, which buttresses the spirit of community. The group also brandishes nationalistic credentials. As described in the previous section, "La Tuta" Gómez Martínez emphasized his willingness to open a dialogue with Calderón. After all, he told the interviewer, "We only want peace and tranquility" and advocate "a national pact" to restore order.[95]

Mass Communication.

On November 22, 2006, La Familia began to communicate openly with the public. It purchased four display ads in two Michoacán newspapers, *La Voz de Michoacán* and *El Sol de Morelia*. In these insertions, it underlined that its "mission" was to "bring order" to the state by eradicating telephonic and direct extortion, murder-for-hire, and the sale of methamphetamines.

In a subsequent interview, two cartel leaders told a reporter that La Familia had been organized 2 years earlier, that it boasted more than 4,000 members, that "strong strategies represent the only way to ensure order in the state," that it provided credits to campesinos, and that it was greatly concerned about Michoacán's youth. They also stressed the imperative to impose basic rigid discipline on criminals, while promising not to bother hardworking, honest people. "We wish to make it known that we are not a menace to society."[96]

Immediately after a grenade attack on September 15, 2008, a possible act of terrorism took place for the first time since the revolutionary period. Around 11 p.m., as thousands of citizens celebrated Independence Day in Morelia, miscreants heaved two fragmentation grenades into the crowd. When the smoke had cleared, eight people lay dead, and more than 110 men, women, and children had been injured. TV networks beamed video footage of the gory scene to incredulous viewers across the country. La Familia immediately used electronic mail, short message service (SMS) text messages, and placards to accuse Los Zetas and the Gulf Cartel of this venal act and to promise "to achieve justice" for the victims of the tragedy. One of its messages stated: "The suffering of the Michoacán people grips us. No more crimes against innocent people. The Zetas will pay for their acts of terrorism. Sincerely, F.M."[97] La Familia presented itself as the "good" (local) cartel versus the "bad" (outsiders).[98]

The Gulf Syndicate responded with its own communiqués in the form of banners draped in prominent spots in Puebla, Reynosa, Cancún, Oaxaca, and Nuevo Laredo. The cartel proffered a $5 million reward in dollars, euros, or another currency to anyone who could help capture members of the La Familia who allegedly produced the mayhem: "The Gulf Cartel energetically condemns the September 15 attack against the Mexican people. We offer our aid for the arrest of the leaders who call themselves 'La Familia'."[99] The *narcomantas* specifically mentioned Moreno González, Jesús Méndez Vargas, and Enrique "El Kike" Tlacaltepetl—big shots within their nemesis.[100]

The Gulf organization followed up this challenge by placing a red ice chest in the center of Lázaro Cárdenas. The head of a La Familia member was packed inside the container next to which a green poster proclaimed: "Greetings Chayo, Rogaciano, and Chango [reference to La Familia's leaders]. This is for the collection of queers who support the terrorists of La Familia; we do not kill innocent people; we kill terrorists like this one . . . [illegible] we don't kidnap and we want neither to work with you nor to have contact with you and those you rely on . . . thanks for those who are supporting us. Sincerely: Gulf Cartel 100%."[101]

Not to be outdone, the Sinaloa Cartel castigated both Los Zetas and La Familia, claiming that "we have never killed innocent people, much less in public events." The syndicate's e-mail communiqué went on to say that the "Sinaloans have always defended the people, we have respected the families of capos and small drug couriers, we have respected the government, [and] we have respected women and children." The message, signed by Mayo Zambada and El Chapo, also expressed a determination "to retake the Michoacán *plaza* and kill all who have offended the Sinaloa family."[102] La Tuta's phone conversation with a TV host signaled a more active stage in La Familia's communications strategy.

Narcocorridos.

As they do with other cartels, balladeers sing the praises of La Familia. This music glorifies the syndicate's leadership, praises its devotion to Christian principles, applauds its contributions to the community, and vilifies Los Zetas. An anonymous singing group has recorded *Jefe de familia michoacana* (Chief of La Familia Michoacana) as the background music for a video. Interspersed with frames that portray narco-banners are others that depict masked soldiers hefting menacing weapons and chasing innocent people, Christ with a halo around his head, a priest celebrating a Mass, a man bathed in sunlight with his arms raised worshipfully to the sky, the five bloody heads lying on the Sol y Sombra nightclub floor, a corpulent prisoner who had a large "Z" carved on his abdomen along with other engravings on his stomach and thighs, and a mean-looking bulbous-nosed judge wielding his gavel with an American flag in the background.[103]

There are also *narcocorridos* and *narcovideos* that link La Familia to Jesús Malverde, the alabaster-skinned, mustachioed "Narco Saint." During the rule of Porfirio Díaz (1877-1911), Malverde became a folk hero because, like Robin Hood, he allegedly stole from the rich and gave to the poor. His admirers insist that agents of the ruling caudillo hung the bandit and left him to rot. Historians have found no convincing evidence that Malverde existed. Nevertheless, there is a crude shrine to his memory on the outskirts of Culiacán. Journalist and author Sam Quiñones reports that: "Smugglers come to ask Malverde for protection before sending a load [of drugs] north. If the trip goes well, they return to pay the shrine's house band to serenade the bandit or place a plaque thanking Malverde for 'lighting the way' . . . ."[104]

Brutality.

Such propaganda aside, authorities attributed 17 decapitations to La Familia in 2006 alone. Between the murder of Rodríguez Valencia earlier that year and December 31, 2008, the syndicate killed scores, if not hundreds, of people. In 2009 there were 370 executions in Michoacán, up from 333 slayings the year before. In 2009 Michoacán ranked high in decapitations (18), which placed it behind only Guerrero (37), Chihuahua (33), and Baja California (24). In terms of tortured victims, Michoacán (97) came in second to Chihuahua (101), while the state led all others in messages attached to corpses (99).[105] Most of the targets of brutality were police officers or members of another narco-band.

It remains to be seen whether this syndicate chopped up the corpse of a 36-year-old man in Los

Mochis, stuffed pieces of his body in different containers, and sewed a soccer ball onto the victim's skinned face. The location of the atrocity suggests another cartel may have sought to surpass La Familia in unspeakable acts.[106]

In mid-2010 Miguel "El Tyson" Ortiz Miranda, a captured La Familia activist, described the training of the organization's potential hitmen. He said that group of 40 are taken to Jesús del Monte, a mountainous zone, and are directed to pursue, shoot, and cook 15 victims. This exercise tests whether recruits can conquer their fear and overcome the sight of their quarries' blood.[107]

Amid rampant brutality that instills fear in the population, social scientists like Carlos Antonio Flores Pérez, an analyst formerly with the Center of Investigation and National Security, Mexico's version of the CIA, say that La Familia's public condemnations of certain ills have helped it gain ground through what is effectively "psychological warfare," and win social legitimacy in a state plagued by violence. "[La Familia] is instituting its own actions to build social roots," said Flores Pérez. "It's a strategy to win over the goodwill of the people in areas in which it operates."[108]

At least some *michoacanos* have bought into La Familia's message that the troublemakers, the killers, and the bad guys are outsiders — not locals or, heaven forbid, La Familia itself. "I applaud the emergence of La Familia Michoacana," wrote one Morelia resident on his blog, adding that he thought the group's presence would result in a 70-percent drop in extortion, drug dealing and kidnapping — another crime that La Familia publicly frowns upon, but is said to engage in.[109]

RESOURCES

La Familia abounds in resources, a large portion of which derive from transforming precursor chemicals into methamphetamines, which enjoy increasing popularity in the United States. The quantities of cocaine, heroin, and marijuana captured during Project Coronado show a flow of dollars from diverse drugs.

Drug Revenues.

Jaime Cervantes Álvarez, a captured member who oversaw production, said that the organization invests one-million pesos (approximately $83,000) to produce 100 kilograms of drugs, which generate 3.5 million pesos ($290,000). Cervantes Álvarez claimed to receive 20,000 pesos ($1,540) for each batch that he processed.[110]

On March 9, 2010, the Mexican Army found a laboratory that contained 10 chemical production units ("reactors"), three times larger than any facility previously discovered. The military confiscated a ton of amphetamines and 300 kilograms of ice, worth approximately $10 million (120 million pesos). Also seized were large amounts of sulfuric acid, caustic soda, and tartaric acid. The megalab was located in Pichátaro, an ecotourism region in the north-central Michoacán.[111]

In 2006 the Mexican government prohibited the sale of products containing ephedrine and pseudoephedrine, major ingredients for methamphetamines. La Familia sent operatives to the Netherlands, Bulgaria, and China to acquire cargoes of amfoleric acid (AFA), another substance that could be converted into meth.[112]

In the same year, the Michoacán-based Cartel, which then claimed 4,000 members, paid its local drug vendors between $1,500 and $2,000. In Morelia alone, there were 1,500 small distributors—with 16,000 sellers in the entire state. These vendors reportedly sold 16 kilograms daily, generating earnings of at least 4 million pesos per day.[113] One expert on La Familia, who asked to remain anonymous, estimated that the syndicate generates hundreds of millions of dollars in gross earnings with the following portions coming from each drug: methamphetamines (50-55 percent), cocaine (25 percent), heroin (15 percent), and marijuana (10 percent).

Extortion.

Extortion also fattens La Familia's secret bank accounts. The owner of a timber business shuttered his operations and laid off workers rather than pay the $600 per month that the syndicate demanded. La Familia acquires resources by selling protection to merchants, loggers, local gangs, small-scale drug sellers, and street hucksters. It takes reprisals against vendors in the underground economy whose contraband clothing, CDs, films, and other items don't carry the "M" logo provided by the cartel. When vendors of pirated diskettes in the Valle de Bravo in Mexico State informed authorities of La Familia's extortion, members of the criminal organization returned to advise them: "For complaining to the police, the monthly quota that you must pay this time is 30,000 pesos and [an additional] 10,000 pesos per month." When arrested, the brigands told law enforcement agents: "We come in a peaceful manner. We are neither kidnappers nor gangsters. We come to restore order and help those whom you cannot."[114]

José Infante, a hotel owner in Apatzingán and head of the local hotel association, says that many hotel owners face demands for monthly "protection" fees and have been told by La Familia not to provide lodging to Federal Police. "We are between a rock and a hard place," he said.[115]

Rather than speak in terms of extortion, the cartel maintains that it "protects" its clients.[116] While 20 percent of businesses nationwide hand over protection money to cartels, the figure is believed to be substantially higher in Michoacán.[117]

Until his capture on December 31, 2008, the chief operative in Morelia was Alberto "La Fresa"/"The Strawberry" Espinoza Barrón, who spearheaded drug trafficking, extortion, and kidnapping in the state capital, as well as cocaine and precursor drugs entering Mexico through Lázaro Cárdenas. La Fresa relied heavily on spies or *puntas* to keep an eye out for the Army, police, and other enemies.[118]

In late April 2009, authorities arrested La Fresa's successor, "El Cede" Cedeño, who—as mentioned earlier—indoctrinated new members of La Familia. In addition to this function, he also oversaw the transport of drugs from Central America; managed the importation of pseudoephedrine from Asia and Europe through Lázaro Cárdenas; extracted payments from bars and night spots where high-school-aged prostitutes plied their trade; participated in indoctrinating new Family members; and organized protests against the military's presence in the state. La Familia unfurled banners that warned: "The people are tired of this military invasion. We are living in a state of siege." At the time of his capture, "El Cede" carried a credential that identified him as a "permanent observer" of the State Commission on Human Rights.[119]

After "El Cede" was taken into custody, his brother, Daniel Cedeño Hernández, stepped down as a federal deputy candidate in the mid-July 2009 election. He had been nominated by the small Mexico Green Ecological Party, which is renowned for irregular practices.

Kidnapping.

La Familia has honed its ability to maximize profits from kidnapping. A naturalized American citizen living in the Chicago area received a cell phone call in September 2009. The voice on the other end of the line said: "We have your father. Try to get the money [demanded] together as soon as you can so that your dad can be freed." The son protested that he could not raise the five-figure ransom. The man, a member of La Familia, replied: "All right, well, if you don't love your dad, then that's fine. We'll just kill him." The cartel clearly had information on the finances of the call's recipient, as well as that of his four brothers and two sisters who also lived in the United States. In the course of four communications over 4 days, the kidnappers sought to spur the family to action. "Try harder." "Put your all into it," "You can do it." The son managed to speak with his father, who said that he was sure La Familia would execute him if a deal was not struck. Finding the Michoacán government hopeless in terms of assistance, family and friends raised the money to liberate the older man. Eventually, the father was released with a broken nose, his eyes taped shut, broken ribs, and a knot on his head from being pistol whipped. "Mexico is like a relative that isn't there," observed the son who spearheaded his dad's freedom.[120]

Businesses.

Often using pseudonyms, La Familia owns scores of businesses in Michoacán. Among these are restaurants, auto parts outlets, pharmacies, hardware stores, auto washes, bars, nightclubs, and convenience stores. Kidnappings and car thefts supplement its bulging bank accounts.[121]

Legal scholar Buscaglia asserted that there are few businesses in Michoacán not affected by traffickers.[122] Another specialist puckishly added that "the cartels are to Michoacán what Boeing Aircraft is to Seattle."

Ovaciones, a mass-market newspaper filled with sports news and photos of half-nude buxom sexpots, reported that La Familia has gotten into the consumer loan business. Reportedly, the organization approves loans within 72 hours at an interest rate lower than banks charge. Within a week of the transaction, customers allegedly receive a communication stating: "Thank you for your trust, now you're a part of La Familia Michoacán."[123] It also collects loans, according to a single mother in Morelia. She contacted La Familia when a man tried to defraud her over the sale of a piece of land. "They told him he had so much time to pay me. He paid, and he won't bother me again," she added.[124]

Weapons.

La Familia has amassed enormous stocks of weapons that it uses both against foes and to intimidate politicians, policemen, and businessmen who refuse to cooperate with the organization.

Its accumulation of resources from methamphetamines, heroin, cocaine, marijuana, and myriad criminal activities has enabled La Familia to amass potent arsenals. Figure 3 indicates several of the arms stores that authorities have found.

Site of Arsenal and Date Discovered	Agency Discovering Cache	Weapons Found	Other Items
Mazamitla, Jalisco July 25, 2010	State Police	Nine fragmentation grenades, 7 AK-47s, 4 short arms, 43 launchers of different calibers, 2,310 rounds of ammunition for AK-47s.	Two vans; and six members of La Familia.
Boundary of the D.F.'s Gustavo A. Madero delegation and the Mexico states slum of Nezahualcóyotl July 14, 2010	D.F. Secretariat of Public Security	Twelve assault rifles, including six AK-47s; two pistols (Beretta 9mm. and .38 Super); a long-range telescopic sight; 43 launchers; and more than 200 cartridges of various calibers.	Authorities captured Kevin Hernández Catalán, 20, who was transporting the weapons.
Apazingán, Michoacán March 25, 2010	Federal Police	Eight assault weapons; two semi-automatic pistols; a fragmentation grenade; and 15 bullet-proof vests.	A dozen state PGR shirts; 5 ski-masks; 15 camouflage pants; and 77 military-type jackets; 4 cell phones; license tags from Wisconsin, Texas, Michoacán, and the D.F.; and three presumed La Familia members: Noé García Durán, 38, Simón Espejo Mendoza, 22, and Urbano Valencia Vargas, 19.
As part of "Permanent Program to Combat Narco-traffic," seizures took place in Apatzingán, Buenavista, Tomatián, Felipe Carrillo Puerto, and Parácuaro Late 2009	Army (Using a GT-200 molecular detector)	Two AK-47s, with 9 loaders; 74 bullets; eight 9 mm. weapons and 171 bullets; three 38-caliber super revolvers with 7 launchers and 35 bullets; three 9 mm. submachine guns with 8 launchers and 27 bullets; two 22 mm. submachine guns; 5 22 mm. rifles; two pistols with a cargador and 56 bullets; nine firing scopes; 2 carbines; and a musket.	$121, 360; military clothing; credit cards, a passport, a driver's license, membership cards, and military service credential.
La Unión, Gro. (near Lázaro Cárdenas) Early November 2009	Navy (Marines)*	19 heavy arms (AK-47s, AR-15s, MAK 90, Berretta 50 caliber; 9 short arms; 14 fragmentation grenades; 134 launchers; 4,606 rounds of ammunition; and	Two bullet-proof vests; 9 ski-masks; and 29 *equipos de fornitura.*
Apatzingán, Michoacán October 29, 2009	Army and Federal Police (AFI)	25 short arms; 4 AK-47s; 36 loaders for AK-47s; 12 loaders for AR-15; 5,000 rounds of ammunition	Military-style clothing; 174 vats (200 liters each) of Phenyl acetic Acid, 20 sacks of Sodium Anhydrous Acetate, and 5 tanks of Freon gas—used for manufacturing meth.
Morelia, Michoacán August 19, 2009	Army	2 pistols (.38 caliber); a hand-held grenade launcher; 8 AR-15s; 3 .38 Super short arms; 15 tear-gas grenades; and 5 fragmentation grenades; more than 1,000 rounds of ammunition; 40 loaders.	Pick-up truck; Ford Explorer; and bumper stickers bearing the words "La Familia Michoacana"; and an iron with the letter "F" used to brand livestock.
Ixtapaluca, Mexico State Mid-June 2009	Federal Police	AK-47 and AR-15 weapons; launchers; pistols; and ammunition	1½ kilograms of cocaine in bricks; 4 vehicles; radios; and motor scooter.

Figure 3. La Familia's Major Arsenals Discovered in 2009 through mid-2010.

orelia, Michoacán ril 18, 2009.	Federal Police	3 AR-15 rifles, a Kalashnikov, 5 grenades, six pistols, a trove of ammunition, and 4 bags containing marijuana and cocaine.	Law-enforcement agents seized these items in a raid that accomplished the capture Rafael "El Cede" Hernández and 43 other members of La Familia, who were attending a party celebrating the baptism of El Cede's grandson.

*The 19,328 Marines form part of the Mexican Navy.

Sources: "Incautan armamento de la Familia Michoacana en Guerrero," *Milenio.com*, November 11, 2009; "Aseguran arsenal de La Familia en Michoacán," *El Siglo* (Durango), October 30, 2009; "Ejército y Policía Federal asguran arsenal en Michoacán," *Noticieros Televisa*, October 30, 2009; and "Elementos de Ejército aseguran en Morelia armas con calcomanías con el nombre de 'La Familia,'" *Notimex*, August 20, 2008; Graham Keeley, "Mexican Police Arrest 44 in Baptism Raid on Drugs [sic] Cartel," *Timeson-line*, April 21, 2009; María de la Luz González, Con detector mo-lecular aseguran arsenal y dinero," *El Universal*, January 1, 2010; "Caen 3 de 'La Familia' en Apatzingán," *El Economista*, March 26, 2010; "Ciudad de México: Confiscan arsenal destinado a La Familia Michoacana: 12 rifles de as alto; 6 AK-47 y 2 pistolas," *El Mundo*, July 15, 2010; and "Caen 6 de 'La Familia' en Jalisco," *Reforma*, July 26, 2010.

**Figure 3. La Familia's Major Arsenals
Discovered in 2009 through mid-2010. (cont.)**

CONFLICT BETWEEN LA FAMILIA AND LOS ZETAS

Although La Familia became an archenemy of Los Zetas in 2006, it adopted many of the paramilitaries' sinister techniques. This *zetanización* includes intimida-tion by brutally torturing victims, castrating them and placing their penises in their mouths, mutilating, and even beheading them; accomplishing hit-and-run ambushes of adversaries; employing psychological warfare by unfurling banners in public places and leaving threatening notes next to cadavers; paying youngsters to serve as lookouts; and complementing drug activities with extortion, human trafficking, kidnappings, murder-for-hire, loan sharking, and dominance over contraband sales by street vendors, and the murder of small drug dealers who spurn cooperation.[125]

La Familia, which intimidates and bribes customs officials, has sought to expel Los Zetas from Lázaro Cárdenas.[126] However, in late 2009, the paramilitaries sought to regroup in Uruapan under the leadership of the former commander of the Municipal Police, Gabriel "El Papí" Espinoza. Other reported leaders of the local cell are Arturo "El Ánfora" López Pérez and a man using the nom de guerre, "El Jamaico."[127] Los Zetas are believed to have retained cells in the port city, and the clash over the port further exacerbates the animus between the two criminal organizations. Amid a rash of slayings in the summer of 2008, Federal Police apprehended Zeta activist Alfredo "El Chicles"/"L-46" Rangel Buendía, who was impelling the battle against La Familia for control of drug routes in the Valle de Toluca and Mexico State municipalities adjacent to the Distrito Federal. Rangel Buendía admitted that one of his missions was to assassinate El Loco Moreno González and El Chango Méndez Vargas.[128] In the same vein, before his arrest, La Familia's Francisco Javier "The Camel" Torres Mora specialized in killing and kidnapping elements of Los Zetas and the Beltrán Leyva brothers in Guerrero.[129]

In what amounted to a declaration of war, "narco-banners" — presumably installed by La Familia — blossomed on pedestrian bridges and along main thoroughfares in five Michoacán municipalities (Morelia, Pátzuaro, Acutzio, Lázaro Cárdenas, and Apatingán) and two towns in Guerrero (Coyuca de Catalán and Tlalchapa) on February 1 and 2, 2010.

La Familia used the same technique to admonish Los Zetas to stay out of Guanajuato. In addition to Salvatierra, León, San Miguel de Allende, and Guanajuato city, the homemade pennants sprouted in 11 other municipalities in the state.[130] These messages emphasized that La Familia was battling "evil beasts" ("*bestias del mal*") on behalf of the nation's law-abiding people and invited citizens to join in this struggle. One poster, scrawled in red and black crayon, proclaimed that La Familia was acting against Los Zetas, the Gulf Cartel, and the Milenio Cartel, indicating that La Familia would become the Guanajuato Family, the Guerrero Family, and, ultimately the "New Familia Michoacana will now become the Mexican [Family] against Los Zetas [and other criminal elements]. Sincerely. La FM [Familia Michoacana]."[131]

La Familia was correct about the presence of their rivals in Guanajuato. In early February 2010, the armed forces captured five presumed Zetas in the Valle de Santiago, 50 miles south of the state capital. Their hideout contained grenades and assault weapons. Guanajuato's attorney general claimed that the men belonged to a well-organized cell.[132]

Los Zetas responded with vengeance to this challenge. On February 5, Michoacán ministerial police discovered five decapitated bodies near Apatzingán, a La Familia stronghold. Los Zetas were the likely executioners inasmuch as the cadavers bore anti-Familia messages: "Follow your Yupo (unknown epithet) and all the dogs of La Familia" and "greetings to frey." "Sincerely, Los Z." The killers had carved the letter "Z" in the backs of two of the dead men's torsos.[133]

During the next 2 weeks, the clash between La Familia and Los Zetas produced 21 decapitations. On February 10, the killers had not only beheaded three victims, they cut up their cadavers, marked them with the letter "Z," tossed them in black plastic sacks, and left them in a street in Morelia.[134] The number of dismembered and/or beheaded corpses totaled 77 during the first 3 months of 2009.[135]

Even though Cárdenas Guillén is serving a 25-year sentence in the United States,[136] he communicated by cell phone with his former pupil, El Chango Méndez Vargas. He argued, in effect, that "Nazario Moreno González was a religious nut and would self-destruct; thus, El Chango should cast his lot with the El Chapo and El Coss,"a Gulf Cartel bigwig. This conversation resulted in an October 2009 venture, which found La Familia sending 500 men to fight Los Zetas alongside the Sinaloa and Gulf Cartels in the North. On August 20, the Army captured four La Familia hitmen, who are believed to have participated in the seizure and murder of Edelmiro Cavazos, the mayor of Santiago, a popular tourist suburb of Monterrey.[137]

In addition to its foray into border states, La Familia has also dispatched a handful of its killers to join a contingent of Sinaloans who have attacked Los Zetas in Veracruz. In return for this action, El Chapo allowed La Familia to use the Sinaloa Cartel's routes to bring cocaine from Guatemala to Michoacán and, then, on to the U.S. — without paying a transit fee; in return, La Familia is instructing his cartel in the construction and operation of sophisticated meth labs.

As astute analysts observed: "The Zetas and La Familia have grown into trafficking powerhouses since Calderón became president. They have altered the playing field by employing methods once unthinkable, such as beheading or dismembering rivals and then displaying their remains in squares, on street corners and in other public places."[138] Figure 4 provides a comparison of the two criminal enterprises.

Characteristics	Los Zetas	La Familia
Origins	Gulf Cartel boss Osiel Cárdenas Guillén, now in prison in the U.S., enticed members of GAFEs to become his body guards and enforcers in the late 1990s.	Emerged from "La Empresa," formed in 2000 by Carlos Rosales Mendoza—with important roles played by José Jesús "El Chango" Méndez Vargas and Nazario "El Chayo"/"El Más Loco" Moreno González
Leadership	Heriberto "El Lazca" Lazcano Lazcano and Miguel "El 40" Treviño Morales); secondary leaders include: (1) Jesús Enrique "El Mamita" Rejón Aguilar/Nuevo León; (2) Raúl Lucio "El Lucky" or "Z-16"/Veracruz; (3) Omar "El 42" Treviño Morales/Northern Coahuila and So. Nuevo León; (4) Galindo "El Mellado" Cruz or "El Z-9" Mellado Cruz/Monterrey; and, (5) José Alberto "El Paisa" Zárate González/Reynosa	"El Chango" Méndez Vargas and "El Chayo"/"El Más Loco" Moreno González. Other key figures include: (1) Enrique "Kike" Plancarte Solís—main coordinator for narcotics sales to U.S., (2) Servando "La Tuta" Gómez Martínez—key public relations man; (3) Dionisio "El Tío" Plancarte—an alcoholic and drug-user who works in public relations; and (4) Ignacio "Cenizas" Rentería Andrade—Uruapan plaza boss who is under indictment by a U.S. court.
Organization	One ranking plaza or cell boss in areas where they conduct operations (his financial operator, who collects the receipts of illegal activities each day, may be a woman, who reports not to the plaza boss but to El 40); under each plaza boss, there will be a number of estacas—according to the size of the venue. Each estaca has 5 or 6 operatives; although all *estaca members kill, the various* estacas in a state or large city may have different specialties—that is, kidnapping, extortion, prostitution, contraband, human smuggling. One member of each *estaca* serves as a lookout. *Plaza* bosses enjoy considerable leeway as long as they meet their financial goals.	25 to 50 plaza chiefs, many of whom control several municipalities; each plaza boss has a number two operative who serves as an enforcer.
Areas of operation	Most of coastal and interior states—with less penetration of the Northwest where the Sinaloa Cartel is dominant; U.S.—mainly Los Angeles, Houston, Dallas, and Atlanta.	Michoacán, Guerrero, El Bajío, Mexico State, the D.F.; present in scores of U.S. cities; Central America; and Europe via "El Wencho."
Identity	Brutal soldiers.	Residents of Michoacán who seek to protect the vulnerable population of the state from outside cartels and gangs.

Figure 4. Comparison of La Familia and Los Zetas.

Ideology	Strict discipline arising from military background of founders.	A perverted fundamentalist Protestantism used as an artifice to attract alienated, unemployed, uprooted young men, who may also have drug and alcohol addiction, into a community—namely "La Familia." Requires new recruits to clean up their lives before they are accepted into the fold.
Drugs Sold	Cocaine, heroin, marijuana, and some meth.	Major meth processor and seller; also cocaine, heroin, and marijuana; only sell marijuana and cocaine in Mexico.
Number of members	Several hundred recruited from ex-military, police, and drug/alcohol addicts from across the country (although principally in the north), as well as *kaibiles*.	A few thousand—with emphasis on recruiting *michoacanos*, including young men who receive treatment at La Familia's rehabilitation centers.
Alliances	Situational alliances with the Beltrán Leyva brothers; see material in next column about the possible emergence of two loose coalitions. El Chapo has courted La Familia since late 2009. He allows them to use the Sinaloa Cartel's routes to bring cocaine from Guatemala to Michoacán and, then, on to the U.S.—without paying a transit fee; in return, La Familia is instructing his cartel in the construction and operation of sophisticated meth labs. Although imprisoned in the U S., Cárdenas Guillén has persuaded "El Chayo" to send 500 men to fight Los Zetas alongside the Sinaloa and Gulf cartels in the North; La Familia has also dispatched a handful of its killers to join a contingent of Sinaloans in attacking Los Zetas in Veracruz.	An arrangement with Juan José "El Azul" Esparragosa, who allowed them to move into Guanajuato without a fight. As a result of the Gulf Cartel's attempting to recapture Nuevo Laredo and Tamaulipas from the Zetas, a working alliance has formed among (1) La Familia, (2) the Sinaloa Cartel, (3) the Gulf Cartel, (4) the Guadalajara Cartel, (5) the weak Milenio Cartel, and (6) shards of the Baja California band once operated by the imprisoned Eduardo Teodoro "El Teo" García Simental. This grouping, which calls itself the "Fusion of Anti-Zeta Cartels" is battling (1) Los Zetas, who are linked to the (2) divided Beltrán Leyva organization, (3) the weak Juárez Cartel, and (4) remnants of the decimated Arellano Félix Organization.
Non-narcotics activities	Kidnapping, murder-for-hire, extortion, contraband, human smuggling, loan sharking, stealing and selling petroleum products, prostitution, businesses, and, possibly, harvesting victims for their body parts.	Kidnapping, extortion, contraband, human smuggling, robbery, loan sharking; mineral theft; businesses; although not involved directly in prostitution, La Familia extorts cash from pimps.
Level of violence	Extremely high, as evidenced by its executing family members of the fallen Marine who was involved in the attack on Arturo Beltrán Leyva.	Extremely high.

Figure 4. Comparison of La Familia and Los Zetas. (cont.)

Training	Green Beret-type instruction, carried out in the organization's camps in Mexico and Guatemala.	Less rigorous military training except for potential gunmen, who—in groups of 40—must track, shoot, stab, and cook 15 victims; intense indoctrination that may take 6 to 8 weeks of lectures, videos, and other teaching devices.
Propaganda	*YouTube*, narco-banners, *corridos*, decapitations, newspaper ads, young people and senior citizens paid to mobilize anti-military/Federal Police operations, and threatening notes left alongside corpses.	La Familia uses the same propaganda techniques; in addition, it kills, tortures, and humiliates alleged criminals.
Involvement of Women	Los Zetas use "*Las Panteras*" to cut deals with authorities, whom they may kill if discussions do not crystallize; also, employed to handle the funds in many plazas; in these cases, they report to "El 40" rather to plaza boss.	Few female members; one exception is Leticia Martínez Guzmán who assists her husband Armando Quintero Guerra in the syndicates' financial transactions.
Social Work	None. Los Zetas want to inspire fear through extreme cruelty rather than cultivate the image of Godfather-types who help the community.	Cosmetic road, church, lighting improvements to attempt to win local favor; small loans to farmer; low-interest credits; uses muscle to collect loans for a fee.

Sources: Manuel Olmos, "Caen seis integrantes de 'La Familia Michoacana,'" *La Prensa*, July 30, 2009; "Cártel del Golfo pierde un brazo," *EXonline*, February 4, 2010; "'Narcoguerra" en Michoacán llega a 21 decapitados este año," *El Universal*, February 20, 2010; and Rolando Herrera and Karla Portugal, "Detallan ataques contra Bautista," *Reforma*, July 1, 2010.

Figure 4. Comparison of La Familia and Los Zetas. (cont.)

DUAL SOVEREIGNTY

The abundant resources described above have enabled La Familia to establish what the late historian Crane Brinton described as "dual sovereignty."[139] In the case of Michoacán, this means that parallel to the elected government stands a narco-administration that generates employment (in growing and processing drugs), keeps order (repressing rival cartels), performs civic functions (repairing churches), collects taxes (extorting businessmen), and screens newcomers to the municipality (employing lookouts). Moreover, the Mexican Constitution prevents mayors, state legislators, governors, and other officials from seeking reelection; no such provision applies to underground leaders, but bullets from opponents rather than ballots may abbreviate their terms.

They also intimidate politicians, many of whom—especially in the Tierra Caliente region—have begun wearing bulletproof vests on a regular basis. In the November 2007 municipal contests in the state, contenders for mayor of Múgica and Nueva Italia stepped aside after receiving death threats. In Coalcomán, Aguililla, and Tumbiscatío, the paramilitaries barred opponents of their favored standard-bearers from voting. José Vázquez Piedra, the outgoing mayor of Turicato who won a seat in the state legislature, said that the imprimatur of the most powerful cartel in drug-infested areas was crucial to winning a public office. The same situation exists in Apatzingán.[140] In late September 2010, assassins shot the interim municipal president of Tancitaro and his companion, increasing to 11 the number of mayors killed nationwide during the year. At least one attractive gubernatorial prospect in a north-central state decided not to enter the race in 2009, lest he place his family in harm's way.

Like other cartels, La Familia shows a great interest in municipal elections because it wants politicians who will protect—or close their eyes to—import activities, processing facilities, local commercial routes, and storage compounds. Should it back a candidate for the Chamber of Deputies, it represents an investment more than the hope of a proximate pay-off; that is, the cartels are counting on the deputy's returning to his state as a prosecutor, secretary of government, mayor, or governor—positions important to their industry.

Even ex-mayors become targets if they are suspected of cooperating with La Familia's enemies. In early-April 2009, authorities discovered the tortured, bullet-riddled body of Nicolás León Hernández, who had twice served as interim municipal president of Lázaro Cárdenas (1984 and 2001). A note left behind read: "This is for all who support Los Zetas. Sincerely FM [Familia Michoacana]."[141]

La Familia has extended its reach into Mexico State, where it controls or has conducted operations in more than a dozen major municipalities. The cartel also operates in Jalisco, Guanajuato, Nayarit, Morelos, Nuevo León, Tamaulipas, and the D.F..

As indicated by the May 26, 2009, arrests, La Familia Michoacana zeroes in on Michoacán politicians, especially local officials who represent municipalities along their trafficking routes. A protected witness avers that, in the 2006 election, the criminal band contributed 2 million pesos ($155,000) to favored mayoral candidates who, if elected, received a stipend of 200,000 pesos ($15,000) per month. The same anonymous source swore that Gubernatorial Contender Leonel Godoy raked in $300,000 from each of La Familia's leaders—a charge he vehemently denies. [142]

In 2009, La Familia began to pay attention to candidates for the Chamber of Deputies. The Attorney General's Office suspected that the cartel was backing aspirants in Apatzingán, Lázaro Cárdenas, Morelia, Pátzcuaro, Uruapan, and Zitácuaro. Its alleged tactics included infiltrating nongovernmental organizations (NGOs), providing funding, and mobilizing street vendors and other groups under its control in behalf of its candidates. By becoming involved in congressional contests, the syndicate could extend its ability to exert political control from the grassroots through the state capitals to the federal government.[143]

La Familia's expenditures on campaigns represent a drop in the bucket compared to the organization's earnings from methamphetamine alone. According to a laboratory operator, the organization invests approximately 1 million pesos ($77,000) in a plant to produce 100 kilograms of ice weekly, which can generate earnings of 3.5 million pesos ($270,000).[144] Federal forces uncover 215 labs in 2009, many of these were in Apatzingán, nestled in the humpback hills of the remote Sierra Madre Mountains, which hide marijuana and opium poppy farms, landing strips for light aircraft hauling cocaine from Colombia, and the increasingly sophisticated methamphetamine laboratories.[145]

At the beginning of his administration, President Calderón dispatched large contingents of Federal Police and military personnel to fight La Familia and other cartels in Michoacán. Calderón even visited the 43rd Military Zone in Apatzingán, a no-man's land of narco-activities in Michoacán. There, he donned a floppy military tunic and sported an olive-green field hat bearing five stars and the national shield—all symbols of the commander-in-chief—to underscore his solidarity with the federal forces assigned to confront drug traffickers. All-in-all, the chief executive launched seven operations in Michoacán. (See Figure 5 for federal government operations.)

Michoacán I	Dec. 10, 2006	Initial deployment of 6,784—4,260 Soldiers, 1,054 marines, 1,420 federal police, and 50 detectives.	To eradicate drug cultivation and to combat by land, sea, and air Los Valencia, Los Zetas, and La Familia; marijuana and poppy fields destroyed, weapons seized, boats and vehicles confiscated and 1,301 suspects arrested, including Alfonso "Ugly Poncho" Barajas, a low-level leader of a Zeta unit.
Michoacán II	Spring-Summer 2007	4,579 federal police and soldiers.	To curb murders and kidnappings as gangs warred over drug routes.
Michoacán III	Oct. 20, 2007	100 members of the military, the AFI, and the PFP.	To stymie narco-activities in the state, with a focus on the port of Lázaro Cárdenas through which cocaine and precursor drugs pour into Mexico.
Michoacán IV	July 28, 2008	Federal police and soldiers from the 21st Military Zone.	To stem the contagion of kidnappings that had reached 30 by late July 2008, compared with 33 during all of 2007; Army confiscated high-powered weapons, ammunition, and fragmentation grenades, while dismantling a house that served as the operations center of the extortionists.
Michoacán V	Sept. 15-16, 2008	Soldiers from the 21st Military Zone, federal, state, and local police.	To restore order and apprehend the culprits who threw two fragmentation grenades into a large crowd in Morelia amid the Sept. 15 Independence Day celebration.
Michoacán VI	May 27, 2009	Federal forces swept into Michoacán, focusing on Lázaro Cárdenas and trafficking corridors from the port. They arrested 32 officials, including 12 mayors.	To disrupt narco-trafficking in this violent state and to demonstrate that public servants involved with cartels did not enjoy impunity.
Michoacán VII	Mid-July 2009	Government dispatched more than 5,500 federal forces to the state, raising the total number to 8,300.	In retaliation for the arrest of "La Minsa" Rueda Medina on July 11, 2009, La Familia launched 21 attacks on Federal Police in Michoacán Guanajuato, and Jalisco, including hotels in which they were staying; on July 13, the blindfolded and tortured bodies of a dozen federal agents, including one woman, were discovered in a bloody heap near the town of La Huacana in south-central Michoacán; all told, at least 17 Federal Police and 2 soldiers perished in the mayhem.

Figure 5. Federal Government Operations in Michoacán.

After the first five armed incursions into the state, Calderón changed his strategy to focus on politicians who were enabling La Familia and other cartels to act with impunity. Pressure from Mexico City forced the February 2009 resignation of Citlallí Fernández González, a former state legislator who was Michoacán's secretary of public safety. She was required to step down because of her lack of success against cartels and her possible ties to La Familia. She then became an adviser to PRD Governor Leonel Godoy Rangel. On May 27, 2009, federal authorities arrested Fernández González as part of a stunning thrust against 32 public officials in Michoacán, including the 12 mayors whose names appear in Figure 6.

Municipality	Mayor	Political Party	Influential Cartel(s) in municipality	Reported Criminal Activity in municipality	Killings in 2009
Apatzingán	Genaro Guizar Valencia	"For a Better Michoacán" Coalition of PRD-PT-Convergencia	La Familia, Los Zetas/Gulf Milenio	Largest meth laboratory in the country	10
Aquila	José Cortéz Ramos*	PRI	Los Zetas/Gulf	In early May, Marines eradicated nine marijuana fields	0
Arteaga	Jairo Germán Rivas Páramo**	PRI	La Familia and Los Zetas/Gulf	A paramilitary attacked the mayor and struck several of his staff	0
Buenavista	Osvaldo Esquival Lucatero*	"For a Better Michoacán" Coalition of PRD-PT-Convergencia	Los Zetas/Gulf	Police attacked with grenades in town of Razo de Órgano	5
Ciudad Hidalgo	José Luis Ávila Franco***	PAN	Los Zetas/Gulf	None reported	0
Coahuayana	Audel Méndez Chávez*	PRI	Los Zetas/Gulf	None reported	0
Lázaro Cárdenas	Mariano Ortega Sánchez	"For a Better Michoacán" Coalition of PRD-PT-Convergencia			
Tepalcatepec	Uriel Farías Álvarez***	PRI	Los Zetas/Gulf and Milenio	Mayor's brother Juan José considered a key lieutenant of Los Valencias	1
Tumbiscatio	Adán Tafolla Ortiz***	PAN-PRI-PVEM	Los Zetas/Gulf and Milenio	None reported	0
Uruapan	Antonio González Rodríguez***	PAN-PANAL	Los Zetas/Gulf, La Familia, and Milenio	In Aug. 2008, Maribel Martínez, secretary of the municipality was kidnapped.	14
Zitácuaro	Juan Antonio Ixtlahuac Orihuela	PRI	Los Zetas/Gulf	In March, the Army captured eight men with AK-47s and AR-15s	0
Múijica	Armando Medina Torres	PRI	La Familia	N.A.	N.A.

Figure 6. Public Officials Arrested in Michoacán.

*Released June 29, 2009.
**Released August 16, 2010, along with Vitorino Jacobo Pérez (security director in Arteaga) and José Lino Zamora (lawyer), and Israel Tentory García (agricultural adviser); 4 days later, former prosecutor Lorenzo Rosales Mendoza gained his freedom.
***Released January 29, 2010.

Source: "Ligan a Alcaldes con 'La Familia'" ("Mayors Linked to 'La Familia'"), *Reforma*, May 27, 2009; "Nombres de los 27 Detenidos" ("The Names of the 27 Arrested"), available from *El Universal.com*, May 26, 2008; Attorney General's Office, Press Release 567/09, May 27, 2009; Azucena Silva and Rafael Rivera, "Cae alcalde de Lázaro Cárdenas, ("Mayor of Lázaro Cárdenas Falls"), *El Universal*, June 30, 2009; Antonio Baranda and Abel Barajas, "Libran ex ediles nexo con el narco" ("Ex Local Officials Linked to Narco-traffickers Freed"), *Reforma*, January 30, 2010; "García Luna niega disculpas a alcaldes" ("García Luna Refuses to Apologize to Mayors"), *El Mañana*, February 4, 2010; Alexandra Olson, "Mayors' Release a Setback in Mexican Drug War," *Associated Press*, March 4, 2010; Elly Castillo, "Liberan a tres ex servidores más del caso 'michoacanazo'" ("Three More Ex Public Officials Freed in 'michoacanazo' Case"), *El Universal*, August 17, 2010; and "Queda libre uno más del 'michoacanazo'" ("One more of the 'michoacanos' is set free"), *El Universal*, August 21, 2010.

Figure 6. Public Officials Arrested in Michoacán. (cont.)

In addition to Fernández González and the mayors, the federal forces took into custody various municipal security directors (Arteaga and Tumbiscatío), ranking law enforcement personnel (Lázaro Cárdenas, Morelia, and Zitácuaro) as well as state public servants (chief of advisers to the attorney general, the economic development director, police agents, and the head of police training). A spokesman for the Office of the Attorney General (PGR), who eschewed the idea of political motivation, stressed that the strike was nonpartisan and derived from intelligence amassed by SIEDO. In provincial areas, there are few secrets about the conduct of public figures. The focus was on Lázaro Cárdenas and trafficking routes from the port. Even though several cartels absorbed hits, La Familia's allies took the brunt of the assault.[146]

In 2007, Uriel "El Paisa"/"The Confidant" Farías Álvarez, brother of "The Grandfather" and a PRI stalwart, won a landslide victory for the mayoralty of Tepalcatepec, which—along with Aguililla, Apatzingán, and Buenavista Tomatlán—graces a drug-smuggling corridor that connects the Tierra Caliente with Jalisco. He dismissed the idea that he or his relatives had ties to the underworld: "My brother only kept a lookout on orders of the Army. And as a result they said he was a narco."[147] Federal forces took El Paisa into custody, along with nine other mayors, on May 27, 2009.[148]

The arrests sparked a thunderous outcry from Mexico's political nomenklatura. It was one thing for the government to pursue criminals; another thing was rounding up public officials who cooperated with narco-traffickers. For politicians, it was the policy version of penalizing jaywalkers. After all, the syndicates had much more firepower and money than office-holders, who—if they resisted the pressure exerted by the cartels—endangered themselves and their families. The shrillest condemnation of this "occupation" by federal forces came from the leftist-nationalist PRD, the party of Michoacán's state executive, Leonel Godoy. He decried the failure of Calderón to consult with him before "occupying" his state. His colleagues in the nation's Senate chimed in. "We oppose the weakening of the Michoacán government that the people elected at the polls," thundered Silvano Aureoles Conejo, vice-coordinator of the PRD's senators, and an aspirant to succeed Governor Godoy. The head of Mexico's National Human Rights Commission (CNDH) also took the government to task for not notifying Michoacán's chief executive in advance "as a political courtesy."[149]

One reason for not notifying the state government was that Godoy's half-brother, Julio César Godoy Toscano, won a federal deputy's seat from Lázaro Cárdenas. After the election, Monte Alejandro Rubido, then technical secretary of the National Security Council, claimed that the legislator-elect worked closely with La Familia. Allegedly, he was a lieutenant of the organization's spokesman La Tuta Servando Gómez. Within days of his March 2010 swearing-in, W Radio broadcast a recorded phone conversation between the new legislator and his "compadre," La Tuta.[150]

The PRI, which scored a thumping victory in the July 5, 2009, congressional contests, even questioned the effectiveness of troop movements under Calderón. State party president Mauricio Montaya Manzo lambasted the detentions, seizures, and arrests carried out by elements of the federal government over the previous 2 1/2 years.[151]

La Familia sought to drum up support by organizing a convoy of buses to drive hours to Mexico City to protest the arrest of Uruapan's mayor. "I'm just here because they [La Familia] told me to come," said a migrant deported from the United States who is hoping the organization will find him a job in the local police force. "I know they [La Familia] are really crazy. In fact, I think they are sick sometimes, but they are the only people in my town who can help you out if you get in trouble, so that's why I joined the group," he added.[152]

Interior Secretary Fernando Gómez Mont brushed aside the bellyaching and encomiums, emphasizing that the gravity of the situation required "an immediate, frontal, and determined response."[153] Moreover, he made a direct challenge to La Familia: "We are ready for you; deal with authority and not with citizens; we are waiting; this is an invitation to you." Deputies and senators across the spectrum decried this bravado as provocative, which signaled Gómez Mont's frustration over the government's inability to quell drug-incited ruthlessness with large military detachments (he subsequently apologized for his statement). The units may tamp down violence in one area only to face an upsurge elsewhere in what one scholar called a "whack-a-mole" dynamic.[154] Yet, reliance on the Army and Navy was essential in light of the venality and unprofessionalism that infused police departments.

In late January 2010, a court in Guerrero ordered the release of 12 of the 32 public servants (four mayors, three municipal officials, two state functionaries, one judge, one municipal policeman, and one state agent) incarcerated more than 7 months earlier for alleged bonds with La Familia and other criminal groups. The judge determined that there was "insufficient proof" to keep them behind bars. The Michoacán state legislature approved the request of three mayors—Adán Tafolla (PRI/Tumbiscato), Uriel Farías (PRI/Tepalcatepec), and Antonio González (PAN/Uruapan)—to return to their offices. González was unable to enter the Uruapan municipal building, which had been occupied by protesters who accused his administration of stealing millions of dollars through phony contracts.[155] Meanwhile, only a handful of officials remain behind bars, and the rest are awaiting the disposition of *amparos*, forms of injunctions.[156]

For its part, the federal government affirmed that it would continue investigating the freed suspects. Despite a tirade from Governor Godoy about the misuse of power, both Interior Secretary Gómez Mont and SSP Secretary García Luna adamantly refused to ask the liberated mayors for forgiveness, because a probe of their links to narco-traffickers was still underway.[157]

Six months before a late May 2009 foray into the state, federal agents had captured Wenceslao "El Wencho" Álvarez Álvarez, an ally of La Familia who ran an international operation out of Nueva Italia, a Michoacán municipality where, ironically, on November 17, 1938, Lázaro Cárdenas established the first *ejido* of his administration. The late president had promised that the communal farm would serve as a model of progress for the nation. Like many growers in the Tierra Caliente, El Wencho claimed that he produced agricultural crops. He vows to have turned to narco-trafficking to avenge the 1999 kidnapping and murder of his father by a vicious gang, Los Arcila. Led by Jorge Álvarez Arcila, a local farmer, and Daniel Farías, the former warden of the Pátzcuaro prison, these brigands enjoyed impunity as they carried out a dozen kidnappings in the Tierra Caliente between 1996 and 2000.

The PGR has connected "El Wencho" to La Familia. His cocaine network allegedly extended from Colombia through Guatemala, Honduras, El Salvador, Venezuela, and the Dominican Republic, as well as to Atlanta, GA, and other U.S. cities. The U.S. law enforcement experts have linked him to Rosales Mendoza and to Miguel Treviño Morales, the number-two figure in Los Zetas. Álvarez Álvarez called the charges against him "false," insisting that he was only a grower of tomatoes, peppers, mangos, and other crops on land rented by his entire family.[158] Credible official sources insist that El Wencho has worked with Los Zetas, as well as La Familia. For the latter, he moved millions of dollars to Monterrey and Nuevo Laredo before laundering it in Atlanta.

In addition to his underworld exploits, El Wencho also owns—or had an interest in—"Los Mapaches" of Nueva Italia, a second-division soccer team that he purchased for 1 million pesos.[159] The AFI waited to arrest the narco-aficionado until Los Mapaches completed a match against El América of Coapa, a third-division team. The police also took 20 players into temporary custody, several of whom were held 2 or 3 days before being released. The previous October 21, the Mexican Football Federation had disqualified Los Mapaches from league play.[160]

Soon after El Wencho's arrest, the PGR issued a communiqué saying that the team owner "operated an organized crime cell dedicated to the purchase, acquisition, transport, and sale of drugs to the United States and [was also involved in] financial transactions and money laundering related to drug trafficking." Still, his team dedicated its next match to Álvarez Álvarez and the announcer asked spectators to hold hands and pray for the accused, even as two Air Force helicopters hovered over the field. A large sign in the stadium proclaimed the team's official sponsors—Empresas Nobaro, Materiales del Río, Hotel Los Arcos, Agroquímicos Cobián, Pinturas Constitución, Mofles Coria, and Importaciones Nobaro—companies believed to be owned by El Wencho.[161]

Law-enforcement officials remain in danger of assassination. La Familia gunmen armed with high-caliber weapons and grenades assaulted the vehicle carrying Minerva Bautista Gómez, the state's public security secretary, on April 24, 2010. The fusillade, in which 2,000 rounds of ammunition were fired, wounded her and killed two of her bodyguards and two passing motorists. Although surviving the assault, Bautista Gómez resigned her post on August 8, 2010, only to agree to take a leave of absence instead because "one cannot remain indifferent . . . in this moment the citizenry is playing a very important role in security matters."[162] In late June, authorities arrested La Familia member Miguel "El Tyson" Ortiz Miranda for leading the ambush.[163]

"We people of Michoacán have seen worse, and we will get past what happened last night," averred Governor Godoy in an effort to downplay the aggression. More outspoken was Alejandra Galván, who told an Internet news site: "We are tired of so many massacres and the inability of our authorities to control this, Please. Do something now!"[164]

In July 2010 a dozen federal agents died in an ambush on the roadway linking Michoacán to Toluca. They were returning home after completing various weeks of police work in Ciudad Hidalgo. Despite this violence, a crowd of 600 people blocked the Ciudad Hidalgo-Morelia and Ciudad Hidalgo-Irimbo Highways for 2 hours on August 1. Their purpose was to protest the presence of the Army and Federal Police in the eastern part of Michoacán. Most analysts believe La Familia generated this demonstration.[165]

LA FAMILIA AND THE UNITED STATES

Before La Tuta assumed the role, ex-Zeta Loya Plancarte presented himself as the spokesman for La Familia. The 53-year-old Michoacán native, who managed press and public relations for the organization, contended that through kidnappings and executions the cartel is ensuring "a peaceful climate for law-abiding citizens." In addition, he cited as his cartel's principal targets, El Chapo Guzmán and the Beltrán Leyva brothers, because they were responsible for methamphetamine addiction in Michoacán communities."[166] It is ironic that La Familia is now cooperating with El Chapo's Sinaloa Cartel in the jihad against Los Zetas in the north. See Figure 7.

Postion	Arellano Félix Organization	Juárez Cartel	Sinaloa Cartel	Gulf Cartel	Beltrán Leyvas	Milenio Cartel	La Familia	Total
Leaders	1	1	2	1	1	1	0	8*
Financial Operators	1	3	15	16	8	0	7	50
Lieutenants	4	5	6	30	8	1	11	66
Hitmen	312	76	240	930	252	30	338	2,178
Corrupted Officials	67	11	30	387	59	0	64	618
Small-scale drug sellers	8,744	11,834	16,217	16,354	8,850	1,503	1,321	64,823
TOTAL	9,129	11,930	16,510	17,718	9,178	1,534	1,741	67,743

*This number includes Zhenli Ye Gon, one of the leading dealers in synthetic drugs.

Source: Aurora Vega, "Suman en el sexenio 67 mil narcos presos" ("The Number of Narco Prisoners Reaches 67 Thousand during Calderón's Administration"), Excélsior, January 15, 2010.

Figure 7. Drug-Related Arrests during Calderón Administration through January 1, 2010.

The religious zeal of La Familia manifests itself in its preference for executions over negotiations. So strong is the organization that it appears to have achieved dominance in Michoacán, eclipsed Los Zetas in Mexico State, crossed swords with the Beltrán

Leyva brothers in Mexico State, ousted a faction of the Sinaloa Cartel from Guanajuato, and blocked other syndicates from entering Michoacán through Guerrero. As Figure 7 indicates, the organization has suffered the capture of 1,741 operatives, including 11 lieutenants. But three-fourths of these arrests have involved small frys; a half-dozen top leaders have fallen during the Calderón administration. Despite the presence of more than 8,000 federal forces in Michoacán, the syndicate continues to conduct business as usual.

Once satisfied with doing business in Mexico, La Familia has moved aggressively into the U.S. market. Although the criminal organization uses several routes, it frequently transports methamphetamines and other drugs in small vehicles from Lázaro Cárdenas to Morelia via Arteaga, Nueva Italia, and Uruapan. In the state capital, the organization transfers the drugs to hidden compartments smothered under fruits, vegetables, and electronic equipment. From there, the shipment usually proceeds through Guanajuato, Querétaro, San Luis Potosí, Zacatecas, Durango, and Mazatlán (Sinaloa) on the Pacific Coast through the Northwest en route to Tijuana, where the goods cross into California. Before his arrest on August 1, 2009, Miguel "La Troca" ("Spanglish" for "The Truck") Berraza Villa, recruited by La Minsa Rueda Medina (who previously performed this function), handled the transfer of drugs from one country to another. He, and presumably his successor, worked with approximately 40 men apportioned among three teams: one that transported the drugs from Michoacán to the border; another that smuggled the narcotics into the United States; and a third squad that received shipments and sold the substances in America.

The export operation has become easier since La Familia no longer has to pay a toll to the Sinaloa Cartel to pass through the "Golden Triangle" of Sinaloa, Durango, and Chihuahua; the *michoacanos* have also cut a deal with the much weaker Arellano Félix Organization to gain access to Baja California. In addition to Tijuana, La Familia also dispatches its shipments of meth northward through Mexicali, Baja California's capital, located 116 miles to the east. Another transit point is Ciudad Juárez, Chihuahua, across the border from El Paso, TX, and then onto Houston, TX, and Atlanta. The raging Gulf-Zeta war in the northern states makes this corridor too dangerous, at least in the short run. As mentioned earlier, thanks to the imprisoned Osiel Cárdenas's influence over El Chango Méndez Vargas, La Familia is cooperating with the Sinaloa and Gulf Cartels in this deadly inter-syndicate battle.

Once across the border, the drivers head for Atlanta, Houston, or Los Angeles. The presence of 3.5 million Michoacán natives north of the Rio Grande enhances the traffickers' ability to sell and recruit lookouts and couriers in these cities, as well as use these metropolitan areas as hubs from which to supply smaller communities.

In 2007 and 2008, DEA officials began receiving inquiries from law-enforcement agencies on both coasts about "La Familia," a cartel that was unknown by most local police departments. In fact, a multiagency Special Operations Division, comprised of more than 300 agents and analysts from federal, state, and local law-enforcement organizations, was hard at work on Project Coronado, which was designed to weaken the Michoacán-based cartel's activities in the United States. Planned for 44 months, the operation culminated on October 22, 2009, and constituted the mightiest blow against a Mexican criminal organization. Coronado involved the arrest of 303 individuals linked to La Familia in the United States, as well as the seizure of 500 kilograms of marijuana, 350 kilograms of methamphetamines, 62 kilograms of cocaine, 144 weapons, 109 automobiles, and $3.4 million in cash. According to the U.S. Justice Department, the investigation was spearheaded by an alphabet soup of agencies—the DEA, the Federal Bureau of Investigation (FBI), Immigration and Customs Enforcement (ICE), the Internal Revenue Service (IRS), U.S. Customs and Border Protection, the U.S. Marshals Service and the Burerau of Alcohol, Tobacco, Firearms, and Explosives (ATF), as well as attorneys from the Criminal Division's Narcotic and Dangerous Drug Section.[167] So far, U.S. authorities have not announced the names of any big shots from La Familia rounded up in the fall strike.

A federal indictment handed down on November 20, 2009, alleged that a Chicago-based criminal organization conspired to distribute cocaine for La Familia, described as a "command and control group" run by "Individual A" (possibly "La Tuta" Gómez Martínez). The manager of the Chicago operation, Jorge Luis Torres Galván, and the distribution supervisor, José González Zavela, reportedly kept in regular contact with their Michoacán interlocutor, keeping him abreast of financial transactions and obtaining approval for wholesalers with which the group could do business. That González Zavala was permitted to sell cocaine on consignment and receive payments once the entire load was sold was a sign of remarkable trust between the parties. "It was likely a matter of the LFM [La Familia Michoacana] commander in Mexico authorizing their involvement and probably was based on an existing business or extended-family relationship," according to STRATFOR Global Intelligence.[168]

The U.S. Treasury Department followed this action with another bold stroke. On February 25, 2010, its Office of Foreign Assets Control (OFAC) designated "El Chayo" Moreno González, "El Chango" Méndez Vargas, and five lieutenants (Dionicio Loya Plancarte, Servando Gómez Martínez, Enrique Plancarte Solís, José Arnoldo Rueda Medina, and Nicandro Barrera Medrano) as "Specially Designated Narcotics Traffickers." Under the so-called "Kingpin Act," U.S. citizens are prohibited from conducting financial or commercial transactions with these individuals and their organizations. The DEA completed "Operation CHOKE HOLD" in early November 2010. This well executed venture shut down a La Familia distribution cell in Atlanta, and spurred the seizure of 45 suspects, $2.3 million in cash, large amounts of drugs, and a cache of high-powered weapons. This action has placed the cartel on the defensive, according to recently captured Lázaro Cárdenas plaza boss, Sergio "El Amarillo"Moreno Godínez. One business immediately affected was the Transportadora Purepecha trucking company, which Barrera Medrano either owns or controls.[169]

CONCLUSION: STEPS TO CURB LA FAMILIA'S ABILITY TO EXPORT DRUGS TO THE UNITED STATES

Even though a backlash is developing, forceful military interdiction of La Familia is especially important because of the irreparable harm that methamphetamines inflicts on addicts. Meth not only injures the user, but can damage infants who have been exposed to the drug before their births. Moreover, it can be transported in smaller-sized containers than, say, marijuana or cocaine, and thus is more difficult to detect.

What can be done to curb the activities of La Familia?

1. *Reinforcement of Present Policies*: The Mexican government must: (a) continue the focus on politicians and businessmen in league with gangsters; (b) improve the gathering and analysis of intelligence through technology and human assets; (c) devise secure programs to encourage and protect informants; (d) identify specific hotspots of drug movement, especially in those specific ports, airports, train terminals, and routes that are heavily used; (e) develop more systematic forensic accounting systems to reduce the flow of laundered funds; (f) embed U.S. attorneys from the Department of Justice with their Mexican counterparts; (g) accentuate coordination by the U.S. Border Patrol with its Mexican counterparts by zeroing in on the same border areas north and south, changing the zone of operations on a daily basis. With respect to the last point, until Mexican law-enforcement agencies become more professional and reliable, American authorities should share minimal intelligence, lest it flow directly into the hands of the narco-traffickers.

2. *Regional Development Program*. Regional programs should be focused on Mexico's impoverished Pacific Coast states — with emphasis on regional development, concentrating on the Tierra Caliente. As long as poverty, poor health care, and unemployment hang like a Sword of Damocles over the 113 municipalities of this area, many of which are isolated, men, women, and children will respond to religious appeals of a better life on earth; some will link arms with a strong advocate of "divine justice" such as La Familia.

3. *Careful Monitoring of Treatment Rehabilitation Cen-*

ters. Authorities should be vested in a single agency for monitoring these facilities, which are recruiting bailiwicks for cartels. Now there is a patchwork of oversight involving federal agencies (Health Ministry, Ministry of Social Development, and the Mexican Social Security Institute), in addition to state-level agencies that vary from state to state. When everyone is in charge, no one is in charge.

4. *Seek Greater Involvement of Other Countries.* Opinion leaders and even the U.S. general public typically assume that "Uncle Sam" — through the Mérida Initiative and bilateral law-enforcement and military programs — will successfully spearhead the fire brigade that helps Mexico extinguish or, at least, curb the drug-ignited conflagration that rages below the Rio Grande. Such optimism derives — in part, at least — from the Wilsonian view that Washington can successfully tackle intractable challenges outside our boundaries.

Yet there are serious constraints on U.S. influence — largely because of the reactive nationalism that infuses Mexico's political, media, and academic sectors, not to mention traditionalists in Mexico's Ministry of National Defense who resent being tutored by North Americans, no matter how diplomatic and well-meaning the instructor. For example, José Luis Soberanes Fernández, then-director of Mexico's National Human Rights Commission, blamed abuses allegedly committed by Mexican troops on the United States because the White House has "forced" Mexico's Army to take the lead in the local drug war. Such nonsense brings to mind the October 1979 charge that a NOAA aircraft had intercepted a storm named "Ignacio" off Mexico's Pacific Coast, thereby contributing to that country's worst drought in 20 years.[170]

For instance, Mexicans enjoy a productive rapport with France, Spain, Italy, the United Kingdom, and Colombia. The Madrid, Paris, Rome, London, and Bogota regimes should be invited to increase sharing their vast counterterrorism expertise — honed in fighting Basque separatists, radical Islamic movements, the Mafia, the Irish Republican Army (IRA), Colombian cartels, and the Revolutionary Armed Forces of Colombia — with the Calderón administration. Indeed, the Colombia National Police have advised the State Security Agency on strategies to combat the contagion of kidnappings and extortion in Mexico State.[171] Meanwhile, pressure must be brought to bear on regimes in Brussels, Sofia, and other capitals to crack down on precursor exports. Their cooperation on these chemicals will foster greater assistance from Washington on combating increased cocaine deliveries to Europe even as Americans demonstrate a rising preference for psychotropics. Canada, which has been a relatively silent partner in the North American Free Trade Agreement, could do even more to deploy its vaunted Customs and Revenue Agency to help attack money laundering. Chemical treatment of currency could enhance detection.

5. *Greater Reliance on the Mexican Navy*. In view of the Mexican Army's deeply-trenched suspicions of the U.S. military, law-enforcement bodies, and anti-drug agencies, Washington should continue to cultivate the Mexican Navy as an important partner in combating La Familia. The Navy, which is more cosmopolitan, more middle class, more merit focused, and more honest than the Army, has a distinguished record in producing intelligence professionals. In addition, Navy Secretary Mariano Francisco Saynez Mendoza is eager to cooperate with U.S. interlocutors. The Navy's

counterpart to U.S. Seals, buttressed by DEA-supplied information, successfully attacked the bunker of drug lord Arturo Beltrán Leyva in Cuernavaca, Morelos, on December 16, 2009. They penetrated three rings of security to kill the so-called "chief of the chiefs" ("*jefe de los jefes*") of one of the country's most powerful cartels. The presence of its Pacific Command in Manzanillo, Colima, and the presence of another base in Lázaro Cárdenas, contributes to the wisdom of the Navy's playing a greater role in anti-La Familia activities.

6. *Hyper-spectral (or multi-spectral) Technology* (HST). The ubiquity of meth labs, especially in the Arteaga area, argues for the use of HST, which directs a beam of light (laser) at the suspected target. The laser makes the various chemicals on or near the target fluoresce at a specific wavelength, which is then captured by an electro-optical sensor. The sensor data are automatically fed into a computerized database of known chemicals, from which it can be determined whether the chemicals used in the production of meth are present and in what concentrations.

7. *Biometrics/facial recognition/voice stress detection systems*. These systems should be used to screen drivers, especially those who seem agitated, perhaps because they are hauling drugs.

8. *Cooperation with Michoacán Community in the United States*. There are several million Michoacán natives living in America. Their organizations in Los Angeles, Chicago, Atlanta, Houston, and elsewhere provide the proverbial sea in which La Familia can swim. Leaders of local Mexican-American organizations, as well as Catholic priests and Protestant ministers, should be convinced to help to stanch the menace presented by the malfactors from their home state.

9. *Repeat Project Coronado with a blow against La Familia's infrastructure.* The focus should be on safe houses, warehouses, money-laundering facilities, vehicles, weapons, and homes of drug dealers.

10. *Decriminalization of physician-prescribed drugs for personal use.* Although Herbert Hoover called Prohibition "a noble experiment," he—like Franklin D. Roosevelt—favored its repeal. They realized that when segments of the public will pay significant amounts to obtain desired products, suppliers will emerge who are prepared to use violence against competitors for the princely sums derived from illegal sales. Only when serious steps are taken to slash the $30 billion to $50 billion generated annually by the narcotics business will it be possible to weaken the cartels. As the late Milton Friedman, a Nobel Prize-winning economist, wrote: "Illegality creates obscene profits that finance the murderous tactics of the drug lords; illegality leads to the corruption of law enforcement officials; illegality monopolizes the efforts of honest law forces so that they are starved for resources to fight the simpler crimes of robbery, theft and assault."[172]

It is easier to advance proposals than to implement them. Nonetheless, President Calderón must either make more headway with his muscular approach or modify this interdiction strategy during his remaining 2 years in office. Results of the July 5, 2009, congressional election and opinion surveys indicate that the once-hegemonic PRI stands a strong chance to recapture the presidency in 2012.[173] It is doubtful that the self-proclaimed "revolutionary party," which worked hand in glove with the traditional crime syndicates for decades, will show the same commitment as Calderón to crossing swords with these vicious warriors.

ENDNOTES

1. This may explain why the death note indicated that they "do not kill women."

2. James C. McKinley Jr., "Mexican Drug War Turns Barbaric, Grisly," *New York Times*, October 26, 2006.

3. Jorge Carrasco Araizaga and Francisco Castellanos, "Michoacán: La Pesadilla de Calderón" ("Michoacán: Calderón's Nightmare"), *Proceso*, n.d. Special Edition No. 25 (second part), pp. 22-26.

4. I am indebted to James H. McDonald, dean and professor of Anthropology, Southern Utah University, for clarifying the boundaries and characteristics of this zone; McDonald, Electronic mail to author, January 23, 2010.

5. Alejandro Suverza, "El poder de 'La Familia Michoacana'" ("The Power of 'La Familia Michoacana'"), *El Universal*, December 4, 2006.

6. Until the Mexican Navy's Marines killed Arturo Beltrán Leyva in Cuernavaca on December 16, 2009, this organization was commonly known as the ABLs. Since Arturo's brother Héctor took the reins, he has called the syndicate the Cártel del Pacífico Sur (CPS); the organization suffered another blow when its U.S.-born top hit man, Édgar "La Barbie" Valdéz Villarreal, broke ranks to form a competing group, "La Compañía."

7. "Cártel del Golfo pierde un brazo" ("The Gulf Cartel Loses an Arm"), *EXonline*, February 4, 2010; also opposing Los Zetas were shards of the Baja California band operated by the imprisoned Eduardo Teodoro "El Teo" García Simental.

8. Antonio Armenta Miralrío, quoted in Adriana Covarrubias, "Pobladores prefieran callar ante inseguridad" ("The People Prefer to Remain Quiet in Face of the Insecurity"), *El Universal*, November 30, 2008.

9. "Arrecian ataques en Michoacán"("Attacks Intensify in Michoacán"), *Reforma*, December 11, 2008.

10. The data emerged from the Encuesta Nacional de Ocupación y Empleo and appeared in Ivonne Monreal, "La pobreza en Michoacán," *Cambio de Michoacán*," January 24, 2010.

11. Quoted in James H. McDonald, "The Narcoeconomy and Small-town Rural Mexico," *Human Organization*, Vol. 64, No. 2, Summer 2005, p. 117.

12. McDonald, p. 122.

13. Greg Brosnan, "Barbaric Drug War to Test Mexico's New President," *Reuters*, December 1, 2006.

14. William Finnegan, "Silver or Lead," *The New Yorker*, May 2010.

15. Howard LaFranchi, "Mexican state sends more workers to us than it has at home," *Christian Science Monitor*, November 8, 1995.

16. Quoted in Marc Lacy, "Money Trickles North as Mexicans Help Relatives," *New York Times*, November 16, 2009; and Banco de México, "Ingresos por Remesas Familiares" ("Income from Family Remittances"), available from *www.banxico.org.mx/polmoneinflacion/estadisticas/balanzaPag...*

17. Silvia Garduño, "Alerta a Michoacán retorno de paisanos" ("Alert in Michoacán over the Return of Countrymen"), *Reforma*, January 9, 2010; and "Recortan apoyo para migrantes" ("Support for Migrants Cut"), *Reforma*, January 9, 2010.

18."Hallan narcolaboratorio" ("Narco-laboratory Found"), *Reforma*, August 14, 2010.

19. "El capo que apela a la 'justicia divina'" ("The Drug Lord Who Appeals to 'Divine Justice'"), *Reforma*, April 12, 2010; and Fabio Fuentes, "Una mujer de *La Familia*, su perdición" ("A woman of The Family, her perdition"), *El Universal*, December 17, 2007.

20. "Denuncian los Valencia persecución" ("The Valencias Denounce Persecution"), *Reforma*, November 9, 2003; and Elseo Caballero, "Asesinan a sicario del 'Cártel del Milenio'" ("They

murder hitman of the 'Milenio Cartel'"), *Esmás*, December 8, 2006.

21. Agencia EFE, "Police Arrests Familia Michoacana Boss, *Vida*, July 15, 2009.

22. These men were Cipriano Mendoza (or Javier "El Remy" Rivera), Eleuterio Guzmán Ramos, Alberto Guízar Reyes, Marco Aurelio Bejarano Hernández, and José Julio Mendoza Guzmán; "Vinculan a 'Los Zetas' en fuga de Apatzingán" ("Los Zetas Linked to Escape in Apatizingán"), *Reforma*, January 7, 2004.

23. "Ofrece 'El Tísico' soborno a captores" ("'El Tisico'/'The Consumptive' Offers a Bribe to his Captors"), *Reforma*, November 3, 2004.

24. Pablo César Carrillo, "Acusación de narco me da risa" ("Accusation of Narco-trafficker Makes Me Laugh"), *Excélsior*, November 13, 2007.

25. "Like a Church on a Hill," *News-Press* (Ft. Myers), September 26, 1999.

26. "Ubican narcorruta de 'Familia' en EU" ("La Familia's Narco Route Found in U.S."), *Reforma*, July 26, 2009; inasmuch as Mexico outlawed imports of ephedrine and pseudoephedrine in 2008, La Familia has begun purchasing AFA, a drug that can be converted into methamphetamine.

27. Rafael Rivera, "'Boom' carguero en Lázaro Cárdenas" ("Boom in Cargo Shipment at Lázaro Cárdenas"), *El Universal*, December 29, 2008; Rafael Rivera, "Lázaro Cárdenas recibe 550 mil contenedores" ("Lázaro Cárdenas Receives 550 Thousand Containers"), *El Universal*, December 28, 2009.

28. Rivera, "'Boom' carguero en Lázaro Cárdenas" ("Boom in Cargo Shipment at Lázaro Cárdenas").

29. Silvia Otero, "Cambian rutas marítimas para el trasiego de drogas" ("Maritime Routes Are Changed for Drug Shipments"), *El Universal*, April 4, 2009.

30. Abel Barajas, "Ligan con Zhenli un megafraude" ("Zhenli Is Linked to a Mega-Fraud"), *Reforma*, February 22, 2010.

31. J. Jaime Hernández, "Postergan indefinidamente extradición de Zhenli Ye Gon" ("Extradition of Zhenli Ye Gon Indefinitely Postponed"), *El Universal*, February 3, 2010; Hector Tobar, "Mountain of Money Tied to Mexico Drug Suspect," *Seattle Times*, July 25, 2007; and John L. Smith, "Is Meth King Ye Gon Talking to U.S. Authorities?" *Las Vegas Review Journal*, October 2, 2009.

32. "Disputan narcos Manzanillo" ("Narco Traffickers Fight over Control of Manzanillo"), *Reforma*, August 11, 2010.

33. In mid-2009, the AFI evolved into the Policía Federal Ministerial or Ministerial Federal Police (PFM).

34. "Reclutan sicarios para Guanajuato" ("Thugs Recruited for Guanajuato"), *Reforma*, February 1, 2009.

35. "Se adueña La Familia de plaza de Guanajuato" ("La Familia takes Over Plaza/Turf in Guanajuato"), *Milenio*, November 8, 2008.

36. *Ibid.*

37. "Policías de Chalco vinculan a su jefe con 'La Familia Michoacana'" ("Chalco Police Link their Chief to La Familia Michocanana"), *Notisistema Informa*, November 7, 2008.

38. "Seguridad" ("Security"), *Terra*, October 17, 2008.

39. "Disputan 4 cárteles el Estado de México" ("4 Cartels Vie for Control of Mexico State"), *Reforma*, November 14, 2008.

40. *Ibid.*

41. *Ibid.*

42. *Ibid*; and María de la Luz González, "Detienen a otro ex mando por masacre de La Marquesa"("Another Former Leader detained for La Marquesa massacre"), *El Universal*, November 14, 2008.

43. César Díaz, "Acechan a 96 Alcaldes" ("Spying on 96 Mayors"), *Reforma*, February 09, 2009.

44. "Realiza Familia Michoacana limpieza social en el D.F." ("La Familia Michoacana Carries out Social Cleansing in the D.F."), *Milenio.com*, April 6, 2009.

45. Jonathan Tapia, "La Familia quiso entrar a San Pedro" ("La Familia Seeks to Enter San Pedro"), *El Universal*, December 19, 2009.

46. Luis Brito, "Pega pelea de cártels a Guerrero" ("Fight in Guerrero Attributed to Cartels"), *Reforma*, March 15, 2010. Contributing to the mayhem is a blood feud within the ABLs between two lieutenants: La Barbie and Sergio "El Grande" Villarreal Barragán, both of whom are now behind bars.

47. Finnegan, "Silver or Lead."

48. This section benefits greatly from Francisco Gómez, "La Tuta, bajo la guía de un brujo" ("La Tuta is Guided by a Sorcerer"), *El Universal*, November 7, 2009.

49. "'La Tuta,' de professor a capo de la 'Familia Michoacana'" ("'La Tuta,' from Teacher to Chief of la 'Familia Michoacana'"), *Informador.com.mx*, November 7, 2009.

50. *Ibid.*

51. Procuraduría General de la República, "En libertad, María Teresa Martínez Castañeda, madre de Servando Gómez (a) La Tuta" ("María Teresa Martínez Castañeda madre de Servando Gómez aka La Tuta is Freed"), *Comunicado 1004/09*, August 19, 2009; Antonio Baranda, "Cercan a familiares de Servando Gómez," ("Family of Servando Gómez Surrounded"), *Reforma*, December 12, 2009.

52. "Trasladan a la SIEDO a integrantes de 'La Familia Michoacana'" ("Members of 'La Familia Michoacana' are Transferred to SIEDO/Mexico's Intellience Agency"), *Informador.com.mx*, July 28, 2010.

53. María de la Luz González, "Vinculan a hermano de Godoy al narco" ("Godoy's Brother Linked to Narco-trafficking"), *El Universal*, July 15, 2009.

54. Manuel Olmos, "Caen seis integantes de 'La Familia Michoacana'" ("Six Members of 'La Familia Michoacana' Fall"), *La Prensa*, July 30, 2009.

55. "'La Tuta,' de professor a capo de la 'Familia Michoacana'" ("'La Tuta,' from Teacher to Chief of la 'Familia Michoacana'").

56. For the text of the interview, see "Presunto líder de La Familia llama al diálogo" ("Presumed Leader of La Familia Calls for a Dialogue"), *El Universal*, July 15, 2009.

57. For these rules, see George W. Grayson, *Mexico: Narco-Violence and a Failed State?* New Brunswick, NJ: Transaction Publishers, 2009, pp. 29-30; and Jo Tuckman and Ed Vulliamy, "Drugs 'Taliban' Declares War on Mexican State," *The Observer*, July 19, 2009.

58. Quoted in "Pide pacto La Familia; Gobierno responde" ("La Familia Asks for a Pact; the Government Responds"), *Reforma*, July 16, 2009.

59. "Fiscalía de NY presenta cargos contra 'La Tuta', y tres más de 'La Familia'" ("Prosecutor in NY Presents Charges against 'La Tuta' and Three More Members of 'La Familia'"), *Cambio de Michoacán*, October 22, 2009.

60. "Dominar al país, plan de la Familia" ("To Dominate the Country, La Familia's Plan"), available from *www.deyaboo.forumcommunity.net*.

61. "Ejecutan a un hombre en Lázaro Cárdenas, Michoacán, dejan narcomensaje" ("A Man Executed in Lázaro Cárdenas, Michoacán, a Narco-message is Left"), *Milenio.com*, April 18, 2009.

62. "Bajo control de 'Los Sierras': El organigrama del grupo" ("Under Control of 'Los Sierras': An Organizational Chart of the Group"), *El Universal*, January 1, 2009.

63. "El Cártel La Familia, sospechoso del narcoatentado en Michoacán" ("The La Familia Cartel Suspected of Narco-attack in Michoacán"), *E-Consulta*, September 18, 2008, available from *www.e-consulta.com*.

64. "Dan prisión a cómplices de 'La Familia'" ("Accomplices of 'La Familia' Sent to Prison"), *Reforma*, January 30, 2009.

65. Presidencia de la República, "Captura al Policía Federal a cinco presuntos secuestradores de la banda 'Los Jaguares,' vinculados con 'La Familia Michoacana'" ("Federal Police Capture Five-Presumed Members of 'Los Jaguares' Kidnapping Band, Linked to 'La Familia Michoacana'"), *Comunicado 033*, Secretaría de Seguridad Pública, January 29, 2010.

66. Quoted in Alberto Torres and Isaías Pérez, "México — Narcotráfico: Políticos y empresarios, detrás de La Familia que ha capitalizado estrategía anticrimen fallida" ("Mexico — Narcotraffic: Politicians and Businessmen behind La Familia that Have Capitalized on the Failed Anti-Crime Strategy"), *Offnews.info*, July 22, 2009.

67. "Golpear su estructura económica" ("Its Economic Structure Suffers Blow"), *Terra*, July 30, 2009.

68. Quoted in Tuckman and Vulliamy, "Drugs 'Taliban' Declares War on Mexican State."

69. Secretaría de Seguridad Pública, "Captura la Policía Federal en Morelia a Coordinador Operativo de 'La Familia Michoacana' e impede su rescate" ("Federal Police in Morelia Capture the Operating Coordinator of 'La Familia Michoacana' and Prevent His Escape"), *Comunicado 299*, July 11, 2009.

70. Quoted in Alberto Fajardo, "Mexican Troops Fan Out across State Hit by Drug War," *Reuters*, July 18, 2009.

71. Finnegan, "Silver or Lead."

72. This paragraph, taken from an enunciation of La Familia's principles, was prepared by Juan Carlos García Cornejo and translated by Mark Stevenson of the Associated Press; the entire

document appears as Appendix 1 in this monograph; see George W. Grayson, *Mexico: Narco-Violence and a Failed State?* New Brunswick, NJ: Transaction Publishers, 2010, pp. 212-213.

73. Quoted in "Van 28 degollados en agosto 7 estados" ("28 Decapitations in August in 7 States"), *El Universal*, August 30, 2008.

74. Rafael Rivera, "'La Familia' castiga y exhibe a ladrones" ("'La Familia' Punishes and Displays Thieves"), *El Universal*, January 30, 2010.

75. Quoted in Finnegan, "Silver or Lead."

76. Malcolm Beith, "La Familia: Society's Saviours or Sociopaths," available from *Mexidata.Info*, October 20, 2008.

77. See George W. Grayson, The PRI Makes a Comeback in Mexico, *E-Note*, Philadelphia, PA: Foreign Policy Research Institute, July 9, 2009.

78. "La nueva fe de los narcos" ("The Narcotraffickers' New Faith"), *Milenio Semanal*, May 30, 2009; "La Familia da cursos de liderazgo y altruismo a sus integrantes" ("La Familia Gives Courses in Leadership and Altruism to its Recruits"), *La Crónica*, August 28, 2009; and "'El Cede' adiestró a más de 9 mil integrantes de 'La Familia Michoacana'" ("'El Cede' Trains More than 9 Thousand Recruits of 'La Familia Michoacana'"), *Cambio de Michoacán*, April 19, 2009.

79. Finnegan, "Silver or Lead."

80. John Eldredge, "re: Mexican Press—John Eldredge," Electronic Mail to author, August 9, 2010.

81. Ransomed Heart Ministries, "Ransomed Heart is a small ministry devoted to a big message," available from *www.ransomedheart.com/ministry/who-we-are.aspx*.

82. John Eldredge, *Wild at Heart Field Manual*, Nashville, TN: Thomas Nelson Publishers, 2002, p. 42.

83. James H. McDonald, Electronic Mail to author, March 19, 2010.

84. Eldredge, *Wild at Heart Field Manual*, p. 14.

85. El Más Loco, *Pensamientos de la Familia [Thoughts of the Family]*, photocopied, n.d.

86. R. M. Schneiderman, "In Some Ministries, Flock Is Now a Fight Team," *New York Times*, February 2, 2010.

87. "Teme 'La Familia' despliegue en Michoacán" ("'La Familia' Fears a Deployment in Michoacán"), *Excélsior*, June 22, 2009.

88. Quoted in William Booth and Steve Fainaru, "New Strategy Urged in Mexico," *Washington Post*, July 28, 2009.

89. "Disputan 4 cárteles el Estado de México" ("4 Cartels Vie for Control of Mexico State").

90. "Taking on the Unholy Family," *The Economist*, July 25, 2009, p. 34; and Luis Astorga, *Seguridad, traficantes y militares (Security, Traffickers, and the Military)*, Mexico City, Mexico: Tusquets Editorial, 2007, p. 190.

91. Quoted in Finnegan, "Silver or Lead."

92. "Pelean Michoacán Zetas y La Familia" ("Zetas and La Familia Fight for Michoacán"), *Reforma*, September 18, 2008.

93. This section on Father Larios is based on Sara Miller Llana, "In a Drug-Ravaged Part of Mexico, a Young Priest Fights to Keep Youths Out of Gangs," *Christian Science Monitor*, January 19, 2010.

94. "Coloca 'La Familia' mantas contra PF" ("'La Familia' Places Banners against the PF"), *Proceso*, November 27, 2009.

95. "'La Tuta,' de professor a capo de la 'Familia Michoacana'" ("'La Tuta,' from Teacher to Chief of la 'Familia Michoacana").

96. Alejandro Suverza, "El poder de 'La Familia Michoacana'" ("The Power of 'La Familia Michocana'"), *El Universal*, December 4, 2006.

97. Elizabeth Pimentel, "Avierte 'La Familia' sobrar a 'Los Zetas' la muerte de inocentes tras atentado" ("'La Familia' Warns that More Innocents Will Die after the Attack by 'Los Zetas'"), September 19, 2008, *Reporte Digital*, available from *www.reportedigital.com.mx*.

98. This theme is developed in Victoria Malkin, "Narcotrafficking, Migration, and Modernity in Rural Mexico," *Latin American Perspectives*, Vol. 28, No. 4, 2001, pp. 101-128.

99. "'Cártel del Golfo': recompense por captura de autores de atentado en Morelia" ("The 'Gulf Cartel': Offers a Reward for the Capture of the Authors of the Attack in Morelia"), *Milenio.com*, October 4, 2008.

100. Carlos Figueroa, "Aparecen narcomantas en dos estados; ofrecen recompensas por líderes de La Familia" ("Narco-banners Appear in Two States; La Familia's Leaders Offer Rewards"), *La Jornada de Oriente*, October 6, 2008.

101. "Dehan cabeza con narcomensaje en hielera en Michoacán" ("Head with Narco-message Left in Ice Chest in Michoacán"), *La Opción de Chihuahua*, October 24, 2008.

102. "El Chapo and Zambada: Vamos por Los Zetas y La Familia" ("El Chapo and Zambada: We Are Going After Los Zetas and La Familia"), *Proceso*, September 23, 2008.

103. For an incredibly gruesome example of this musical/ photo propaganda, see "La Gran Familia Michoacana," available from *www.youtube.com/watch?v=6DUByKswkS4&NR=*.

104. Sam Quiñones, "Jesus Malverde," Front Line: Drug Wars, PBS, available from *www.pbs.org/wgbh*.

105. Rolando Herrera, "Acelera narco ejecuciones" ("Executions by Narco-traffickers Accelerate"), *Reforma*, January 1, 2010.

106. Olga R. Rodriguez, "Mexico Cartel Stitches Rival's Face on Soccer Ball," *Associated Press*, January 8, 2010.

107. Rolando Herrera and Karla Portugal, "Detallan ataques contra Bautista" ("Attacks against Bautista Detailed"), *Reforma*, July 1, 2010.

108. Quoted in "La Familia: Society's Saviours of Sociopaths?" *Visions of Hosiery*, September 25, 2008, available from *cyanide257. wordpress.com/2008/09/25/la-familia-societys-saviours-or-sociopaths/*.

109. *Ibid.*

110. "Ubican narcorruta de 'Familia' a EU" ("La Familia's Drug Trafficking Route to the U.S. Located").

111. "Descubren 'megalaboratorio' en Michoacán ("Mega-laboratory Discovered in Michoacán").

112. Miguel Cabildo S., "La Familia, líder en producción de drogas sintéticas: SSP" ("La Familia, Leader in Synthetic Drug Production: SSP"), *Proceso*, July 27, 2009.

113. Antonio González Díaz, "México entre dos fuegos" ("Mexico between Two Fires"), Mexicanal, n.d., available from *www.**mexicanal.com**/blog-entry/antonio-gonzalez/17495*.

114. "Paga o muere: tradición de 'La Familia'" ("Pay or Die: The Tradition of 'La Familia'"), *El Universal*, February 22, 2009.

115. Quoted in Sara Miller Llana, *Christian Science Monitor*, November 23, 2009.

116. "Mexico's Hydra," *Security in Latin America*, available from *networkedintelligence.wordpress.com/tag./la-familia/*.

117. Lemic Madrid, "Los extorsionadores se ensañan con la IP" ("Extortionists Enrage the IP/Private Industry"), *Excélsior*, April 1, 2009.

118. Ignacio Alzaga, "'La Fresa' sí era el jefe de la Familia, confirma Sedena" ("'La Fresa'/'The Strawberry' Was Indeed the Chief of La Familia, Confirm Sedena/Defense Ministry"), *Milenio*, December 30, 2008.

119. "Exigío Rafael Cedeño en febrero de 2008 el regreso de soldados a sus cuarteles" ("In February 2008, Rafael Cedeño Demands that Soldiers Return to their Garrisons"), *El Norte*, April 21, 2009.

120. This dramatic episode draws heavily on Meribah Knight, "Families Fear Phone Call from Mexico's Cartels," *New York Times*, July 31, 2010.

121. Jorge Carrasco Araizaga and Francisco Castellanos, "Michoacán: La Pesadilla de Calderón" ("Michoacán: Calderón's Nightmare").

122. "Taking on the Unholy Family."

123. Reported in Carlos Manuel Rodríguez, "Michoacan Drug Cartel Offers Bank Services, Ovaciones Reports," *Bloomberg.com*, September 15, 2009.

124. Quoted in Finnegan, "Silver or Lead."

125. Alejandro Suverza, "El evangelio según La Familia" ("The Gospel according to La Familia"), *Nexosenlinea*, January 1, 2009.

126. "Quitan puerto a 'Los Zetas'" ("'Los Zetas' Driven from Port"), *Reforma*, October 4, 2009.

127. Luis Brito, "Detectan egreso de 'Los Zetas'" ("Exit of 'Los Zetas' Detected"), *Reforma*, December 16, 2009.

128. "Multiplica 'Familia' violencia en Edomex" ("Familia Multiplies Violence in Mexico State"), *Reforma*, September 14, 2008.

129. "Cae presunto jefe de La Familia Michoacana" ("The Presumed Head of La Familia Michoacana Falls"), *Noroeste.com*, April 22, 2009.

130. The other municipalities were Comonfort, Dolores Hidalgo, Silao, San Francisco de Rincón, Jerécuaro, San José Iturbide, Salamanca, Uriangato, Moroleón, Cortázar, and San Luis de la Paz"; see V. Esposa and E. Flores, "Tapiza 'La Familia' Guanajuato, Guerrero y Michoacán con mantas contra 'Los Zetas'" (Tapiza 'La Familia' Hangs Anti-Zeta Banners in Guanajuato, Guerrero, and Michoacán"), *Proceso*, February 1, 2010.

131. *Ibid.*

132. "Militares detienen a cinco presuntos 'zetas' en Valle de Santiago" ("The Military Detains Five Presumed 'Zetas' in the Santiago Valley"), *El Universal*, February 3, 2010.

133. "Hallan a 6 decapitados" ("6 Beheaded Found"), *Reforma*, February 7, 2010.

134. "'Narcoguerra' en Michoacán llega a 21 decapitados este año" ("Michoacán's 'Drug War' Has Produced 21 Decapitations This Year"), *El Universal*, February 20, 2010.

135. "'Calientan' plaza 'Zeta' y 'Familia'" ("The Plaza/Turf of the 'Zetas' and 'Familia' is Heating Up"), *Reforma*, April 3, 2009.

136. The 7 years that Cárdenas Guillén served in a Mexican prison will be deducted from his 25-year sentence; good behavior, especially information to help capture the leaders of Los Zetas, could reduce even further the erstwhile Gulf Cartel leader's time behind bars. When requested by the U.S. Department of Justice, federal judges, under Rule 35 of Criminal Procedure, have exhibited flexibility in shortening the prison time of a cooperative inmate.

137. "Aparece en Nuevo León 'La Familia'" ("'La Familia' Appears in Nuevo León"), *Reforma*, August 21, 2010.

138. Tracy Wilkinson and Ken Ellingwood, "Mexico under Siege," *Los Angeles Times*, August 8, 2010.

139. Brinton, *The Anatomy of Revolution*, New York: Random House, 1938.

140. Pablo César Carrillo, "Elección con tufo a narco" ("Election with the Stench of Narco-traffickers"), *EXonline*, November 17, 2007; and Abel Miranda, "Intimidan a los penales de Guerrero" ("Intimidation in Guerrero Prisons"), *Excélsior*, January 8, 2009.

141. "Executan a ex Alcalde michoacano" ("Ex Michoacán Mayor Executed"), *Reforma*, April 3, 2009.

142. "Dicen que 'La Familia' apoyó campañas" ("It's Said that 'La Familia' Supports Political Campaigns"), *Reforma*, June 20, 2009.

143. Francisco Gómez and Alberto Torres, "'La Familia' quería colocar políticos federales propios" ("'La Familia' Wishes to Elect its Own Federal Politicians"), *El Universal*, May 29, 2009.

144. Francisco Gómez, "'La Familia' extiende sus redes hasta Europa y Asia" ("'La Familia Extends its Network to Europe and Asia"), *El Universal*, July 26, 2009.

145. Brosnan, "Barbaric Drug War to Test Mexico's New President."

146. "Ligan a Alcaldes con 'La Familia'" ("Mayors Linked to 'La Familia'"), *Reforma.com*, May 27, 2009.

147. Quoted in Carrillo, "Acusación de narco me da risa."

148. In the aftermath of this venture, the Secretary of Public Security issued a communiqué about the arrest of other La Familia members: Willibaldo "El Willi"Correa Alcántara (kidnappings and executions); Nicolás "México" Morales González (*plaza* of Melchor Ocampo municipality); Luis Yarza Solano (western Michoacán); Martín "El Cheyas" Sandoval Gómez (Valle de Bravo, Mexico State); José Ángel "Oliveras" Oliveras Marín (bodyguard of Dionisio Loya Plancarte); and Juan "Juan Serna" Herrera Jiménez (purchase and storing of drugs). See "Capturan a seis presuntos integrantes de la Familia Michoacana" ("Six Presumed Members of La Familia Michoacana Are Captured"), *Milenio.com*, June 12, 2009.

149. Jorge Ramos Pérez, "Gobierno debió avisar a Godoy 'por cortesía: CNDH" ("The Government Should Have advised Godoy 'as a Courtesy': CNDH/National Human Rights Commission"), *El Universal*, May 28, 2009.

150. "Aplaude la bancada del PRD el amparo ortogado a Julio Godoy" ("The PRD's Legislative Faction Praises the Injunction Granted to Julio Godoy"), *El Universal*, March 26, 2010.

151. Quoted in Azucena Silva, "PRI critica aumento de fuerzas federales" ("The PRI Criticizes the Increase in Federal Forces"), *El Universal*, July 21, 2009.

152. Tuckman and Vulliamy, "Drugs 'Taliban' declares war on Mexican State."

153. Quoted in Jorge Ramos, "'Legítima defensa' despliege en Michoacán Gobernación" ("Interior Ministry Calls Deployment in Michoacán 'Legitimate Defense'"), *El Universal*, July 19, 2009.

154. Quoted in Hal Brands, *Mexico's Narco-Insurgency and U.S.Counterdrug Policy*, Carlisle, PA: Strategic Studies Institute, U.S. Army War College, 2009, p. 34.

155. Alexandra Olson,"Mayors' Release a Setback in Mexican Drug War," *Associated Press*, March 4, 2010.

156. Antonio Baranda and Abel Barajas, "Liberan ex ediles nexo con el narco" ("Former Local Officials Linked to Narcotrafficking Released"), *Reforma*, January 30, 2010.

157. "García Luna niega disculpas a alcaldes" ("García Luna Refuses to Apologize to Mayors"), *El Mañana*, February 4, 2010.

158. "Entra 'Wencho' al narco en busca de revancha" ("'Wencho' Entered Narcotrafficking in Search for Revenge"), *Reforma*, November 12, 2008; and María de la Luz González, "Mapaches 'lavaron' en siete países" ("Criminals 'Launder' Funds in Seven Countries"), *El Universal*, October 15, 2008.

159. "Paga 'El Wencho' $1 millón por equipo" ("'El Wencho' Paid $1 Million for the Team"), *Reforma*, November 14, 2008.

160. Raúl Ochoa, "Narcofutbolistas, Nueva modalidad de los capos" ("Narco-owned Soccer Teams: A New Venture for the Drug Lords"), *Proceso*, October 9, 2008.

161. F. Castellanos and Raúl Ochoa, "Oran and marchan en defensa de narcoequipo" ("Praying and Marching in Defense of the Narco-owned Soccer Team"), *Proceso*, October 13, 2008.

162. Quoted in "Minerva Bautista aceptaría regresar a la SSP" ("Minerva Bautista Agrees to Return to the SSP/Ministry of Public Safety"), *El Universal*, August 12, 2010.

163. Tracy Wilkinson, "Ex-Police Commander Held in Michoacán Ambush," *Los Angeles Times*, June 30, 2010.

164. Quoted in Tracy Wilkinson, "Gunmen kill 4, Wound Top Security Official in Michoacán," *Los Angeles Times*, April 25, 2010.

165. "Protestan Contra Federales en Michoacán" ("Protests against Federal Police in Michoacán"), *Reforma*, August 2, 2010.

166. Alejandro Jiménez, "Atentados en Morelia Investigan ligas entre alcaldías y 'Familia'" ("Attacks in Morelia Spur Investigation of Ties between Mayors and 'La Familia'"), *El Universal*, September 19, 2008; and Sam Logan and Kate Kairies, "U.S. Drug Habit Migrates to Mexico," *Americas Policy Program Special Report*, February 7, 2007, available from *www.americas.irc-online.org*.

167. "More than 300 Alleged Familia Cartel Members and Associates Arrested in Two-Day Nationwide . . .," *Forbes.com*, October 22, 2009.

168. STRATFOR Global Intelligence, "'La Familia' North of the Border," December 3, 2009.

169. U.S. Department of Treasury, "Treasury Sanctions La Familia Michoacana Leadership," Bulletin TG-564, February 25, 2010; and "EEUU da un nuevo golpe al cartel méxico de la 'Familia Michoacana,'" *Terra*, February 25, 2010.

170. George W. Grayson, *The United States and Mexico: Patterns of Influence*, New York: Praeger, 1984, p. 7.

171. César Díaz, "Asesora Colombia contra plagio en Edomex" ("Colombians provide Advice about Kidnapping in Mexico State"), *Reforma*, March 13, 2009.

172. Quoted in Milton Friedman, "An Open Letter to Bill Bennett," *Freedom Daily*, April 1990.

173. George W. Grayson, "The PRI Makes a Comeback in Mexico," *E-Note*, Philadelphia, PA: Foreign Policy Research Institute, July 9, 2009.

APPENDIX I

LA FAMILIA ENUNCIATES ITS PRINCIPLES

THE MICHOACÁN FAMILY

Who Are We?

Common workers from the hot-lands region in the state of Michoacán, organized by the need to end the oppression, the humiliation to which we have constantly been subjected by people who have always had power, which in turn allowed them to perpetrate all kinds of dirty tricks and abuses in the state. These include members of the Milenio Cartel, those named Valencia, and other gangs, like the Gang of 30, who from the 1980s until today have terrorized much of the state, in particular, the areas of Puruarán, Turicato, Tacámbaro, and Ario de Rosales, and who have carried out kidnappings, extortions, and other crimes that disturb Michoacán´s peace.

Mission.

Eradicate from the state of Michoacán kidnapping, extortion in person and by telephone, paid assassinations, express kidnapping, tractor-trailer and auto theft, home robberies done by people like those mentioned, who have made the state of Michoacán an unsafe place. Our sole motive is that we love our state and are no longer willing to see our people's dignity trampled on.

Perhaps at this time there are people who do not understand us, but we know that, in the areas most affected, they understand our actions, since now it is possible to ward off these delinquents who come from other states and whom we will not allow to enter Michoacán and continue committing crimes. We are eradicating completely from the state the retail sale of the lethal drug known as ice, as it is one of the worst drugs, one that causes irreversible damage to society. We are going to prohibit the sale of altered wine said to come from Tepito. We know that what comes from there is of poor quality.

Objective.

To maintain the universal values of the people, to which they have full right. Unfortunately, to eradicate the ills we have mentioned, we have had to resort to robust strategies, as we have seen that this is the only way to bring order to the state. We will not allow it to get out of control again.

Why Did We Form?

When the Michoacán Family organization began, we did not expect that it would be possible to get rid of kidnapping, paid assassination, fraud, and the sale of the drug known as ice. But, thanks to the great number of people who have had faith, we are achieving control over this great problem in the state.

The Family, as a group of people, has grown, such that at this moment we cover the entire state of Michoacán. This organization sprang from the firm commitment to fight the out-of-control crime that existed in our state. The Family has achieved great, important advances by fighting these problems little by little, but we still cannot declare victory. We can say that the state has seen an 80-percent improvement with regards to these problems. We have also reduced kidnapping by the same percentage.

People who work decently at any activity need not worry. We respect them, but we will not allow people from here or from other states to commit crimes or try to control other types of activities. When we first began to organize and proposed putting an end to the street sale of the drug known as ice, many told us that not even First World countries have been able to get it under control. Nonetheless, we are doing it.

For Reflection.

What would you do as a resident of Michoacán? Would you join the Family if you saw that we are fighting these crimes? Or would you let them proliferate? Give us your opinion.

You, Family man, I ask you: Would you like to see your son out on the streets in danger of getting involved in drugs or crime? Would you support this organization in its fight against the maladies that attack our state?

The media have been responsible and objective in their coverage of events that have occurred. We appreciate their impartiality and thank them for their coverage of our actions.

Other countries have not even seen such organizations formed on the people's behalf, and yet we have already begun. . . . Success depends on the support and understanding of Michoacán society.

Sincerely,

The Michoacán Family
Prepared by Juan Carlos García Cornejo
(Translated by Mark Stevenson, the Associated Press)

APPENDIX II

THE FAMILIA'S LEADERS, MIDDLE MEN, AND OPERATIVES

Name	Background	Function	Relevant Material	Status
		TOP LEADERS AT LARGE		
Moreno González Nazario "El Chayo"	Born March 8, 1970; migrated to No. California as a teenager before returning to Michoacán; arrested in McAllen, TX, for transporting drugs (spring 1994).	Shared leadership of La Empresa with Jesús "El Chango" Méndez Vargas and Carlos "El Tísico" Rosales Mendoza before becoming La Familia's top leader; in charge of overall operations, as well as activities in Morelia.	Mexican government has posted a 30 million peso reward for information leading to his capture; extremely secretive.	At large.
Méndez Vargas Jesús "El Chango"	Born Aug. 6, 1973/Feb. 28, 1974, Gro.	Top leader; in charge of activities in Apatzingán.	Mexican government has posted a 30 million peso reward for information leading to his capture; extremely secretive.	At large.
		TOP LEADER ARRESTED		
Rosales Mendoza, Carlos "El Carlitos"/"El Tísico" (The Consumptive")	Born in El Narajito (municipality of La Unión, Gro.), Feb. 12, 1963.	A founding father of La Empresa, which evolved into La Familia.	Worked with the Milenio Cartel before becoming the lieutenant of Osiel Cárdenas Guillén, Gulf Cartel boss, in Michoacán.	Military arrested him in Morelia, Oct. 24, 2004.
	SECOND	**TIER AT LARGE**	**LEADERS**	
Barrera Medrano, Nicandro "El Nico"	Born Nov. 2, 1964.	Former plaza chief in Uruapan.	Owns Transportadora Purepecha, whose trucks reportedly ship drugs.	At large.
"El Sierra 11"		In charge of San Luis Potosí.		Uncertain; may have been killed on orders of "La Mimsa" Rueda Medina.
Gómez Martínez, Servando "La Tuta"	Born in Arteaga, Mich., Feb. 6, 1966.	Number 3 in leadership and performs public relations for the cartel; major zone of influence is the coast of Guerrero and Michoacán, as well as mountains of Michoacán and the municipality of Arteaga where his brother Flavio is or was plaza chief.	Reportedly ordered the killing of 12 Federal Police known as the "Michoacanazo" on July 13, 2009; Mexican government has posted a 30 million peso reward for information leading to his capture.	At large.
Loya Plancarte, Dionisio "El Tío"	Born Oct. 21, 1955.	Public relations specialist for the organization; however, his excessive drinking and drug use are becoming a liability.	Mexican government has posted a 30 million peso reward for information leading to his capture.	At large.
Méndez Hernández, Alfredo "El Inge"		Former plaza chief in Turicato.		At large.

105

	SECOND	TIER AT LARGE	LEADERS	
Ortega, Jorge "La Gaviota"		In charge of Querétaro.		
Plancarte Solís, Enrique "El Kike"	Born Sept. 14, 1970.	Main coordinator for drug sales to the U.S.		At large.

	SECOND	TIER ARRESTED	LEADERS	
Alamillo Quintero, Alberto Martín "El Alamo"		Top operator in Mexico State	Captured some 20 presumed members of La Familia members, including his closest collaborators: José Luis "El Alacrón" Montes and José Luis "Macoy" Pérez.	Federal authorities captured him and his cohorts in Villa Nicolás Romero, Mexico State, Sept. 2, 2008.
Berraza Villa, Miguel Angel "La Troca"		Took over duties of Arnoldo "La Minsa" Rueda Medina, who was captured on July 11, 2009; La Troca moved meth into the U.S.		Federal Police captured him at a service in the church of Perpetuo Socorro in Apatzingán, Aug. 1, 2009.
Cedeño Hernández Rafael "El Cede"	Born in 1962 or 1963.	Rose from a small-time operator who enforced "derecho de piso" and shook down illegal night clubs, to become plaza chief in Lázaro Cárdenas, with responsibility for imports of precursor drugs; accredited as a permanent observer of the Michoacán State Human Rights; Commission; his ascent in the organization followed the arrest of Alberto "La Fresca" Espinosa Barrón, Dec. 31, 2008.	The chief proselytizer of recruits; claimed to have indoctrinated 9,000 new members in 2008; reported directly to Moreno González.	Federal Preventative Police captured him along with 44 other criminals at a baptism, in Morelia, Apr. 19, 2009.
Espinosa Barrón, Alberto "la Fresa"		Plaza chief in Morelia where he oversaw (1) storage of cocaine and other drugs, (2) shipments via Lázaro Cárdenas, (3) bribery and intimidation of officials; and (4) lookouts or halcones who spied on Army and Federal Police movements.		Army captured him in Morelia, Dec. 31, 2008.
Hernández García, Enrique "El Rizos"		Chief of cells in Mexico State that specialized in kidnapping, extortion, executions, and drug retailing.	Also captured were accomplices, known For kidnapping: Hilda "La Hilda" Camacho Villa-Gómez, and Gerardo "El Taz" Moreno Lozano.	Federal authorities arrested him in Morelia, Dec. 1, 2009.
Larios Sandoval, Jesús "El Kiko"	Born in Apatzingán, Mich., 1968	Along with Kike Plancarte Solís, served as contact for distributing synthetic drugs and cocaine in the U.S.; began his criminal activity at age 17, when he sold drugs and worked at other jobs in California and Texas.	Worked directly for El Chayo Moreno González and El Kike Plancarte Solís with whom he attended school.	Federal Police captured him in Copándaro de Galeana, Mich., Dec. 21, 2009.

	SECOND	TIER ARRESTED	LEADERS	
Medina, José Antonio "Don Pepe"	Born 1974/75	Transported 440 pounds of heroin each month into the U.S. for La Familia.	Known as the "King of Heroin."	Federal Police arrested him in Mich., March 24, 2010.
Ortiz Chávez, Javier "El Arqui"	Born in 1953/54; ex-Ministerial Police officers in Mich.	Top boss in Mexico State—with particular responsibility for Coacalco, Tultepec, Tultitlán, and Ecatepec, as well as the municipalities of Charo and Tzitzio in Mich.	Gen. Rodolfo Cárdenas Cruz said the group was Involved in at least 20 executions, including comandantes and police in Mexico State and Mich.	Federal authorities arrested him and 10 accomplices in raids in Mexico State and Mich., May 27, 2009.
Ramírez Hernández, Víctor Guillermo	Ex-PFP commissioner; five years as police chief in three Guanajuato municipalities: Valle de Santiago; Salamanca, and Apaseo el Alto.	Provided protection to La Familia.		Army and Guanajuato state's Special Immediate Reaction Group (GERI) arrested him in Silao, Gto., June 15, 2009.
Rueda Medina, Arnoldo "La Minsa"	Born Dec. 15, 1969.	Coordinated logistics for producing methamphetamines and exporting cocaine and marijuana to the U.S. and other countries; also designated chiefs in various *plazas* in Michoacán, Colima, San Luis Potosí, Jalisco, Guanajuato, Edomex, and Aguascalientes.	His mid-2009 arrest detonated a four-day revenge battle between La Familia and the military and Federal Police, highlighted by the execution of 12 members of the Federal Police.	Federal Police captured him in his home in Morelia, July 11, 2009.
Sotelo Barrera, Javier "El Pancho"	Born in Lázaro Cárdenas, Mich. in 1991 or 1992.	At the direction of his uncle, he carried out executions, kidnappings and extortion of businesses in León, Gto.	Nephew of "La Tuta" Servando Gómez Martínez; active in mid-July 2009 killing of Federal Police after the arrest of "El Minsa."	Elements of the Guanajuato Attorney General's Office captured him along with four accomplices in Guanajuato, July 15, 2009.
Zamudio Vallejo, Manuel "El Rosky"	Born in Morelia, 1968/69	Planned, coordinated, carried out operations in Mexico State; a vicious killer, kidnapper, and extortionist.	Rose to became boss of Mexico State after the arrest of Javier "El Arqui" Oritz Chávez (May 27, 2009) and Enrique "El Rizos" Hernández García (Dec. 1, 2009).	Federal Police captured him in Cuautitlán Izcalli, Edomex, on/about Feb. 11, 2009.
	LOWER	LEVEL AT LARGE	PERSONNEL	
Armas, Quito "La Cobra"		Plaza chief in Aguascalientes		At large.
Barrera Medrano, Nicario "El Nico"		Plaza chief in Uruapan		At large.
Castañeda Chávez, Ignacio and Ramón		Plaza chiefs in Nocupétaro		At large.
Coria Mendoza, Damile		Money launderer; allegedly linked to the former mayor of Uruapan, Antonio González Rodríguez.		At large.
Godoy Toscano, Julio César		Reportedly in charge of protection network in region of Lázaro Cárdenas, Arteaga, and Nueva Italia; won election as PRD nominee to Chamber of Deputies on July 5, 2010, but yielded seat to his alternate.	Half-brother of Gov. Leonel Godoy Rangel	Serving in Chamber of Deputies.

	LOWER	LEVEL AT LARGE	PERSONNEL	
Gómez Martínez, Flavio		Was or is plaza chief in Apatzingán.	Brother of "La Tuta" Gómez Martínez.	At large.
barra Piedra, Martín		Plaza chief in Parácuaro		At large.
Peñaloza Soberanes, Alfredo and Antonio		Directed hitmen in Lázaro Cárdenas and Ixtapa-Zihuatanego, Gro.		At large.
Solís Solís, Saúl "El Lince"		Interlocutor with business community and local authorities to advance the goals of La Familia; active in the La Huacana region and Mexico State.	Won a seat from Arteaga in the Chamber of Deputies as a candidate of the Mexican Ecological Green Party (PVEM) in the July 6, 2009, election; not allowed to take his seat; and is first cousin of La Familia leader, Enrique Plancarte Solís; arrest warrant outstanding.	At large.

	LOWER	LEVEL ARRESTED/KILLED	PERSONNEL	
Alba Álvarez, Rogaciano	Born in Petatlán, Gro., 1955/56.	Contested control of Petatlán and La Unión, Gro. near Lázaro Cárdenas, with Los Zetas and the Beltrán Leyva organization, which has vowed to execute him and has killed two of his sons and kidnapped his daughter.	Former PRI mayor of Petatlán, Gro. (1993-96) and ex-president of the Association of Live-Stock Producers in Gro.; ties to the Sinaloa Cartel and La Familia.	Federal Police arrested on Chapala-Guadalajara highway, Feb. 11, 2010.
Carmona, Francisco Javier "M60"	Born 1988/89	Believed to serve as head of a cell for four Edomex municipalities; allegedly responsible for 7 murders and 8 kidnappings; SSP indicated that his "modus operandi" was to kidnap victims near their residences or businesses, using powerful weapons and violence and, even if a ransom were paid, to executive their capitives..	Captured with four accomplices: Uriel "El Charras" Flores Sepúlveda; Edgar Alan Felipe "El Marino" Hernández; and María del Conseulo "N"/"Chelo" (wife of "El Charras"; and Francisco José "El Pez" Hernández Ramírez (a member of "Los Peces," a gang linked to La Familia.	Arrested in D.F., March 17, 2010.
Carranza Galván, José Luis "El Jaguar"		Operative in Mexico State		Family members apparently killed him for some transgressions, Ecatepec, Nov. 28, 2008.
Cervantes Montaño, Hugo or Carlos Hernández García "El Tomate" or "El Tomatón"		Operator in the Plaza in Nueva Italia, Mich.	Took orders directly from El Chango Méndez Vargas; among the items found in his possession was bulletproof vest that belonged to a police officer killed in mid-2009 in La Huacana.	Police arrested him in Apatzingán, Jan. 30, 2010.
Cervantes Álvarez, Jaime	Born in Felipe Carrillo Puerto, Mich. 1975/76.	In charge of processing chemicals into meth.		Federal Police arrested him on in Acuitzio, Mich., July 27, 2009,
Fernández Castañeda, Juan Víctor "El Brujo"		Used tarot cards to advise Gómez Martínez; served as lookout and personal aide to "La Tuta."	La Tuta trusted him to handle his bank account and to provide gifts for the capo's girlfriends.	Federal Police captured him in Arteaga, Aug. 16, 2009.

	LOWER	LEVEL ARRESTED/KILLED	PERSONNEL	
Frías Lara, Francisco Javier "El Chivo"		Plaza chief in Petatlán, Gro., (near Lázaro Cárdenas) and head of hitmen in the Costa Grande, which lies above the Tierra Caliente.	Believed to have been operative for ambushing 12 Federal Police Officers on July 13, 2009.	Federal Police arrested him in Petatlán, July 13, 2009.
García Garnica Jorge "El Bofo"		Plaza chief in Zamora, Mich.		Army arrested him in Zamora, Oct. 30, 2009.
Gómez García, Alejandro "El Rojo"		Presumed plaza chief in Carácuaro, Mich.	An informant told the Army of Gómez García's whereabouts.	Army arrested him in Morelia, early March 2010.
Govea Martínez, Ulises Daniel "El Uli"	Born in Uruapan, Mich., 1986/87.	Courier for La Tuta.	Stepson of Armando Quintero Guerra.	Federal authorities arrested him in Uruapan, July 27, 2009.
Hernández Barajas, Valdemar "El Bombón" or "El Once"	Born in 1990/91	Lives with Jessica Bautista Martínez, the niece of La Tuta, who is the young man's political mentor.	Participated in a July 18, 2010, attack in Tizapán el Alto, Jalisco, in which one policeman died and four were wounded.	Jalisco police arrested him in Mazamitla, Jalisco, July 25, 2010.
Hernández Harrison, Miguel Ángel "La Cuchara"/"The Big Spoon"		Specialist in extortion, collecting transit fees ("derechos de piso"), and coordinating clandestine laboratories.		Federal Police captured him at a service in the church of Perpetuo Socorro in Apatzingán, Aug. 1, 2009.
Jacobo Nares, Claudia del Carmen "La Química"		Specialist in producing methamphetamines in Apatzingán and Uruapan.	One of few women in La Familia; she reported directly to "La Tuta" Gómez Martínez and "Kike" Placarte Solís.	Federal Police arrested her in Apatzingán, Dec. 21, 2009.
López Barrón, José Alberto "El Gordo"	Born in Arteaga.	Confidant of "La Tuta" Gómez Martínez; operated a cell in Arteaga; also responsible for marijuana activities in La Cañas, Tumbiscatio, and La Mira.	Reported earning 2,500 pesos ($210) to 3,000 pesos ($250) per week as a lookout.	Federal authorities captured him on the Siglo XXI highway between Lázaro Cárdenas and Morelia, July 13, 2009.
Magaña Mendoza, Luis Ricardo "El 19 1/2"		Responsible for coordinating shipments of synthetic drugs to the U.S.; also involved in extortion, kidnapping, and bribing authorities in Zamora, Jacona, Ecuandureo, and other Michoacán municipalities; plaza chief in Zamora.	Extremely close to "La Tuta" Gómez Martínez.	Army captured him in Manzanillo, Colima, Aug. 23, 2009.
		In charge of security for La Tuta in Arteaga, Mich.		Federal Police arrested him in Arteaga, July 27, 2009.
Martínez Guzmán, Leticia	Born in 1967/68.	Worked with her husband, Armando Quintero Guerra, in financial transactions	One of few women visibly active in La Familia.	Federal Police arrested her in Uruapan, July 27, 2009.
Méndez Alfredo "El Inge"		Plaza chief in Turicato		
Moreno Madrigal, Ramón "El Llavero" or "El Diablillo"		Received cocaine shipments from Colombia through Lázaro Cárdenas.	Reportedly, he held the same rank in the organization as La Tuta; first cousin of Moreno González.	
Ortega, Jorge "La Gaviota"		Plaza chief in Querétaro.		
Ortiz Miranda, Miguel "El Tyson"	Joined Michoacán police in 1999 and became commander of security forces before retiring in 2008 after a murder warrant was issued against him; began working for La Familia in 2005.	Active in Morelia Plaza.	Participated both in the June 14, 2010, ambush of Federal Police in Zitacuaro and attempted assassination of state security chief Minerva Bautista Gómez.	Federal Police captured him in Morelia, June 29, 2010.

	LOWER	LEVEL ARRESTED/KILLED	PERSONNEL	
Oyarzabal Hernández, Héctor Manuel "El Héctor"		Plaza chief in Chalco, Valle de Chalco, Ozumba, Ixtapluca, in Mexico State; supplied small dealers and undertook extortion of merchants and kidnappings.		Federal Police captured him in Chalco, Aug. 15, 2009.
Quintero Guerra, El Licenciado"	Born in Tancítaro, Mich.	Key financial specialist who oversaw revenues from the purchase and sale of drugs in Mexico and the United States; coordinated logistics of drug traffic between Baja California (Tijuana and Mexicali) and Los Angeles.	Captured along with his wife, Leticia Martínez Guzmán, a collaborator in financial transactions, and Lourdes Medina Hernández, 24, presumed fiancée of "La Tuta."	Federal Police arrested him in Uruapan, July 27, 2009,
Pérez Rivas, Ricardo "El Yankee"	Born in Zitácuaro, Mich.; 1982/1983.	Carried out kidnappings of businessmen and drug smuggling in Michoacán, Querétaro, and Mexico State under orders of Rueda Medina before the latter was captured; based in Zitácuaro where he may have been the plaza boss.	Captured also were 18 accomplices, including 10 women (two of whom where minors) and four members of the "Jaguares," a gang that collaborates with La Familia in kidnappings.	Federal Police arrested him and his operatives in Mich., Dec. 3, 2009.
Pineda Pérez, José Juan "El Pineda"		Assisted Genaro Orozco Flores in providing security for "LaTuta.".		Federal Police arrested him in Uruapan, July 27, 2009.
Rentería Sáenz, Daniel "El Reno"	Born in Morelia, 1977/78.	Kept track of funds flowing from drug sales, extortion, and contraband; acquired vehicles, communications equipment, and furnishings for safe houses in Mexico State, Morelia, and other municipalities in Mich.		Federal authorities captured him in Morelia, July 27, 2009.
Torres Mora, Francisco Javier "El Camello"	Born 1966/67	Chief of hitmen who captured and executed members of Los Zetas and the Beltrán Leyva organization in Guerrero.		Federal Police captured him during the baptismal ceremony in which Cedeño Hernández was apprehended in Morelia, April 18, 2009.

Sources: "Violencia en Edomex" ("Violence in Mexico State"), *Reforma,* September 14, 2008; Mario González, "Military Arrests Drug Leader; Military's Role in Drug War Debated," *CNN.com*, December 31, 2008; "Desnuda a 'La Familia'" ("The Family is Denuded"), *El Mundo* (Orizaba), January 2, 2009; "Arrestan a un jefe del narco cartel La Familia" ("A Chief of the La Familia Cartel Is Arrested"), *La Prensa Gráfica*, February 12, 2009; Lemic Madrid, "Anuncian la detención de 44 de La Familia" ("The Detention of 44 Members of La Familia Is Announced"), *Excelsior*, April 30, 2009; Francisco Gómez, "'La Familia' creció por el cobijo oficial: testigos" ("'La Familia' Grows Thanks to Official Protection: Witnesses"), *El Universal,* June 22, 2009; "Confirman nexos de los Godoy con 'La Familia'" ("Ties between Godoy and 'La Familia' Confirmed"), *El Financiero*, July 14, 2009; "La Familia monta guardia en Michoacán" ("La Familia Stands Guard in Michoacán"), *Informador.com.mx,* July 22, 2009; "Policía federal captura 'La Min-

110

sa'" ("Federal Police Capture 'La Minsa'"), *La Voz Nuevo*, July 23, 2009; Manuel Olmos, "Caen seis integrantes de 'La Familia Michoacana'" ("Six Members of 'La Familia Michoacana' Fall"), *La Prensa*, July 30, 2009; "Detienen a 3 miembros de la Familia que operaba en el Edomex" ("3 Members of La Familia Who Operated in Mexico State are Detained"), *Contexto de Durango*, December 3, 2009; "Detienen a 19 integrantes de La Familia Michoacana" ("19 Members of La Familia Michoacana Are Detained"), *Diario de Yucatán*, December 4, 2009; "Frustra 'Familia' arresto de La Tuta" ("'Familia' Frustrated the Arrest of La Tuta"), *Reforma*, December 11, 2009; "Detienen a 'la Química' de La Familia Michoacana" ("'The Chemist' of La Familia Michoacana is Detained"), *El Universal*, December 24, 2009; "Cae líder en el Edomex de 'La Familia'" ("The Leader of 'La Familia' in Mexico State Falls"), *Reforma*, February 12, 2010; "Cae Rogaciano Alba, cacique guerrerense" ("Guerrero Strongman Rogaciano Alba Is Arrested"), *Reforma*, February 12, 2010; "Detenido en Ciudad de México jefe de célula de cártel 'La FamiliaMichoacana'" ("The Chief of 'La Familia Michoacana' Cell in Meixco City Is Captured"), *El Periódico de México*, March 18, 2010; and E. Eduardo Castillo, "Mexico Arrests 'King of Heroin,' with Ties to U.S., *Associated Press*, March 25, 2010.

U.S. ARMY WAR COLLEGE

Major General Gregg F. Martin
Commandant

*****

STRATEGIC STUDIES INSTITUTE

Director
Professor Douglas C. Lovelace, Jr.

Director of Research
Dr. Antulio J. Echevarria II

Author
Dr. George W. Grayson

Director of Publications
Dr. James G. Pierce

Publications Assistant
Ms. Rita A. Rummel

*****

Composition
Mrs. Jennifer E. Nevil

www.ingramcontent.com/pod-product-compliance
Lightning Source LLC
Chambersburg PA
CBHW071157280526
45787CB00002B/534